"DEATH OR LIFE"

the Life of [the true repentance]

Henry Proosa

*Scripture quotations are taken from the "**HOLY BIBLE**" and are marked in "**[ ]**". Mainly is used **Expanded Bible version [EXB]**, unless otherwise noted.*

*There are used **different "HOLY BIBLE" translations**:*

ISV	*International Standard Version*
NLT	*New Living Translation*
GNV	*1599 Geneva Bible*
EHV	*Evangelical Heritage Version Bible*
ASV	*American Standard Version*
ESV	*English Standard Version*
DRA	*Douay-Rheims 1899 American Edition*
NRSV	*New Revised Standard Version*
NIV	*New International Version*
BRG	*Blue, Red and Gold Letter Edition Bible*

All names are named as initials for privacy reasons, except Anre.

I **dedicate** this book to **You**!
That is not a **coincidence** that you are reading this book! It doesn't matter how the book reached to you;
I thank God for you!

"*11 We have much to say about this, but it is hard to explain because **you are so slow to understand** [hard of hearing; ^C spiritually]. 12 By now **you should be teachers**, but **you need someone to teach you again the first lessons** [elementary truths; basic principles] **of God's message** [revelation; oracles]. **You still need the teaching that is like milk** [^L milk]. **You are not ready for solid food.** 13 [^L For] **Anyone who lives on milk is still a baby** and **knows nothing about** [or is unskilled/inexperienced with] **right teaching** [or the message about righteousness]. 14 But **solid food** is **for those who are grown up** [mature]. **They are mature enough** [...who through practice/exercise have trained their faculties/senses] **to know the difference between good and evil.**"
[Hebrews 5:11-14]

Contents

ABOUT 1

    What is this book about? 1

    Why did I write that book? 2

    When did I write this book? 3

    To whom I wrote that book? 4

    Why is that book different from others? 4

    Who am I? 5

BEFORE WE START 6

TESTIMONY 7

INTRODUCTION 12

CHAPTER 1 25

    FIRST VISION 142

    SECOND VISION 144

    THIRD VISION 144

    FINALE BATTLE 146

MEETING GOD IN COURT 152

CHAPTER 2 159

THANK YOU 160

FAVOURITE CONTENTS

Here you can create your own Table of Contents. You could write your **favorite topic** *and page number* **that is mentioned** *in the book so that you could find it quickly*

NOTES	TOPIC	PAGE

ABOUT

What is this book about?

This book is not an **ordinary** book; it is actually based on a **diary** that I named "**Spiritual Warfare.**" It's just **one chapter** from the diary, and it's about **true repentance,** how to live it, and stay in it and so much **more**. Also, it includes some commentaries, brief history, and explanations about situations, etc.

This book is written with boldness and exposing sin and evil's work. There are no illustrations; it's very straightforward and sincere. It also includes lots of **different** and **essential topics** that we experience in our Christian's life: things that we don't want to talk about.

In the end, you may even call it an "**ugly truth of Christian's life.**" "**DEATH or LIFE**" (we rather say "Life or Death", but I emphasize "Death" first) is a fundamental **question** and **a decision** that we all have to make and some point, we do make it; it doesn't matter if we are aware or not, it will be made. Even if we think that we don't, we are already deceived, also "not making the decision" is already **decision**.

And the book shows how little things can turn into big things, and how little things matter more than we could ever imagine. Start with small things, and you will see where it will lead; how things will unfold.

Why did I write that book?

It's easy to say and sounds like a *cliché* that *"God told me."* But I won't say it.

I have thought for years why we do not remember the good works that God has done for us, they will fade over the years, but I have thought that something should be written down and how to do it. Summer 2019, I thought that I'd have to start somewhere. Since the situation in my life was already heartbreaking, and I knew I needed to begin repenting, the Holy Spirit said that I have to start writing a diary; in an old fashion way, with a pencil and new diary. For me, as a man, this is a good challenge because I have not been the kind of person who really wants to write. I had tried to write something before, but there was no discipline or interest, etc. This time I **decided** that I was going to start writing, and I started with a "turning point of my life"; it means, I began to repent of the most important things.

We seek the Truth; we seek the answers to our questions. During this quest, our questions change in the process, they become a *self-sacrificing* from *self-centeredness*, our questions revolve around us; *"I and me"* and *"to me"*, but then they change to *"you"* and *"for you"*. We will get the answers to our questions, but sometimes the questions are wrong, the motives of the questions are wrong.

I **recommend** reading and digesting on each topic calmly; all this information is in a concentrated form and even at times, robust.

We forget God's miracles and what He has done for us, and we can even get used to them, so we take His intervention for granted and lose our gratitude.

As I said: it's my life and testimony and one part of the journey, which is in front of me. I didn't write this book so that people could

copy my life. No, it is only for **encouragement,** and I'm just another **example** and **proof** of what Lord God is doing **today,** that **He** is **Real** and **He loves You!**
I want you to be **fervent**; my heart longs for you. You are in my heart!

When did I write this book?

I started to write the diary in **August 6,2019;** the original diary is in Estonian. I began to digitize it from paper to Microsoft Word, about the beginning of 2020, after the battle inside of me, questioning, " **why**." Sometimes you don't have to know why things happen; you will understand when the time is right, I just had to listen and obey. And then I had a revelation about a dream, and I knew that I have to write it as a book. I can't just keep it to myself, because it's not meant to be.
When **COVID-19** broke loose, I knew **God's timing was perfect**. It is the perfect time to take time off and take a look at where we stand today. Where are we in our search? Where are we in our spiritual road? What is the situation with our soul?
How is our relationship with God?
These situations that shake the world, this panic, **show what is in our hearts**. Are we ready?

To whom I wrote that book?

I believe that God will **instruct**, **direct**, and pulls people to the *truth*. This book is just another way to seek and experience the truth, and it's part of a bigger picture.

I don't want to put people in the boxes as the world does, but there's only one question: " *Could you handle it?*"

It's easy to say that it's only for Christians, but we don't know exactly who are these "true" Christians. Everybody who's wearing the "**Mask of Christianity**" aren't it. It doesn't even matter what situation you are right now (*young Christian, being on the edge of losing faith, religious Christian, tired Christian, suicide thought, disappointed in God, etc.*); **important is where you will go from here.** Essential is that you ask the right questions, and **you seek the Lord God, Jesus Christ, and you want to know them personally.**

What do I want to say? It's not *milk* anymore, it's a *solid* food. You need teeth to chew this book, and if you can swallow, then digestion is even more difficult, but you need to give time.

You even may feel sick in your stomach and want to throw up. But no worries, this is the expected reaction.

But **never give up on your faith in Jesus**!

Why is that book different from others?

Should it even be different? Should we compare it with other books at all? Not really. There's always different messages, points of view and experiences.

There's always "*but*": as I mentioned, that is a diary, it may seem that it's dry and incomprehensible or leads nowhere, but it has **a purpose**.

My recommendation is to read it from beginning to the end, and you will get the picture. There aren't any chapters or Table of Contents like we are used to seeing in books.

I do not doubt that God will speak and reveal things to you. You may call it just one of the "*God's tools*".

Who am I?

Nobody knows me. I have no experience in writing books. I use it as an **advantage**. I never believed that I would write a book, because I have nothing to write about. I always had an opinion that the best writers are those how imagine unrealistic things, and there's nothing to do with real life, and seemed to be ridiculous and a waste of time. But for me: everything changed in 2019. I try to approach from a different angle as I see things, and keep it simple. This book is just a fragment of my life.

My name is Henry, and I'm 35 years old. I've been married nine years to my beloved wife, Maila, and we have two children; both boys, one is two and a half years old, and the other is seven years old.

I am Estonian, and I was born at the end of the Soviet Union; I was seven years old when it collapsed. I still live in Estonia.

I've *considered* myself a Christian for over 25 years, maybe longer. I started to go to church when I was a little boy, both my parents are Christians.

But I've been *living as* a Christian for about five years now.

What do I mean by that?

I mean that there are differences between *considering* myself as Christian or living like a **true** Christian, being in "**covenant with Living Lord God**," and being a "**son of God**". You may define it as "religious Christian." Christian means following Jesus or Jesus' disciples. I didn't refer myself as a **believer**, because everybody believes in something or somebody.

The year **2015** was a very crucial year for me; that's the year when I started to search for the Lord God, and I was **baptized with the Holy Spirit**.

BEFORE WE START

READER'S ATTENTION NEEDED!

In the following: there are **two different boxes** included in the diary:

1.)

Scriptures from the bible (box with gray background)

2.)

Content box (without gray background) that **includes**: My own thoughts, **knowledge**, brief history, explanations of situations, **revelations**, my experiences, **testimonies**, confessions, opinions, **spiritual secrets**, etc.

TESTIMONY

LIBERATION IN NORWAY 2007

Anre

I want to share one of the most important life events and give testimony, which I consider the most important in my life. All that has happened to me prior to that, has been merciful and gracious. He answers prayers, but now I'll tell a story, which shows that God is also a Holy. He never compromises with sin within us.
He yearns that we could be closer to Him, and He wants us as His children to be pure and holy in all that we are.

After returning from Afghanistan, I quit the Estonian Defense Force and went to Norway to do construction work for one year. I was there with my father. We lived in a tiny Norwegian village. We rented a house for two, which was located in such a beautiful place with a nice view of the big mountains and fjords. There really was nowhere to go or anything to do in the village. I had found myself in a forsaken land. I thought it was an excellent opportunity to seek God and get closer to Him. So, I **decided** after the workday to climb a few kilometers up, where there is a beautiful view and where there are no people. We planned to stay in Norway for exactly two months and then come home in the afterwards. I **decided** to go out every night and seek God. I will pray to Him for two months, and then I will see what God will do with me.
My **decision** was so firm that I thought nothing could or should stop me for two months.
It usually took half an hour to climb to the top of the hill.
And for the first month, I prayed every night with a broken heart. I

cried and cried out to Jesus.

But to my great sorrow, I experienced that there was no God in what I was doing. I asked and screamed to Him. The more I prayed, the emptier I felt. After a month of crying and praying, I noticed that I had nothing to pray for. All the things I could think of and ask for were already done. I surrendered to Him, prayed His intervention in my life. I prayed for blessings for myself and for all my friends and acquaintances. I prayed for great awakenings in Estonia, etc.

But I felt that all I had prayed was utterly pointless and useless. I had kind of emptied myself, but received nothing.

Then I wondered and asked God, what's going on, where are You, why can't I hear You, are You angry with me?

Suddenly the Holy Spirit spoke to me directly into my heart and said, *"Be silent and know that I am God!"* The moment I heard these words within me, I knew right away that was God speaking to me. But the words that God spoke were full of deep love and care and there was no condemnation or pressure. These words came as from the King of the Kings, full of Power and Authority. But I still felt embarrassed that I was the only one who was talking all the time!

I didn't give Him a chance to say anything. God was patient with me. He waits for me to pour out myself until I'm empty, so that He may take over. From the next day, I **decided** to be silent and wait for Him. But the next time, after about 10 minutes, I discovered that I was the one who's talking again. I couldn't keep quiet, my thoughts and other soulfulness erupted very strongly. I confess that it required an effort to learn to be silent before the Lord. But I didn't give up. Every day I was able to learn to silence myself more and more until the 40th day of prayer and climbing to the mountain. It was the 40th evening, and I was standing in the same place where I looked down at the valley and thought about God. Then I asked the Lord that today is 40 days full, Jesus was just as much in the desert, and then the devil came and began to tempt Him. So, where is my teaser? Let him come, and I will defeat him also with the Word. But nothing happened. There was silence. Then I asked God to reveal Himself in some way so that I would know that He hasn't forgotten me. Also, nothing happened right away. So, I went home with disappointment. But that same night, I had a bizarre dream.

I saw that I was in my apartment, where I had lived for years. And the ceiling above the apartment had been removed or raised. The most shocking picture was that there stood the altar of Satan. Literally, it was like a demonic place of sacrifice where some living beings were sacrificed. It was very disgusting looking, bloody, and boiled. Human remains, and skulls were floating around. I watched it all and was so shocked and frozen that how it was possible to have such a sermon going on in my apartment ceiling. Then suddenly, I struck this altar with my foot, and I screamed with all my heart that I will break it in the name of Jesus, my Lord. When my foot touched the altar, it was like a bomb exploded. All the pieces flew all around, some pieces flew in my mouth, and I spat it out right away, and I said how disgusting it was.

And then I woke up. I didn't know right away what it could mean. I waited for God every night to reveal its meaning. But then I had the idea to call my good friend, an American pastor, and a missionary to share this dream. So I did, and we prayed together. And he said over the phone that it was probably the sins of my past that still live in me!

As soon as he said that, I realized that these were my sexual sins that remained in my heart.

I hadn't repented for these. My apartment symbolized my heart.

I did not commit these sins externally anymore, but I kept those memories within me.

I loved it. These cases took place years ago—different places with different girls.

I remembered these memories time after time, and I enjoyed and got the satisfaction of thinking and meditating on them.

I realized so clearly what the bible says **[Matthew 15:19 ASV]:**

> *"For <u>out of the heart</u> come forth evil thoughts, murders, adulteries, fornications, thefts, false witness, railings"*

I had worn it with me all along. And it was inside of me – the "altar of Satan" in my heart.

No other thing in my life has fascinated and bound me like the sin of fornication.

I wondered if it was still possible for me, as a child of God, to have an altar of Satan in my heart? When I studied the bible, I discovered that it is entirely possible. In the next days, I began to pray that God would show me specific times and places that I have to repent. And then, after a long wait and silence before the Lord every night, He reminded these situations. And I renounced from all this sin from the past with all my heart, and I repented of that. I'd will judge myself and ask Your forgiveness. I said to God that I rather die if I go back to fornication! And then I bound that memory in the name of Jesus and crushed it with the words so that it would never come back to my mind. As soon as I said those words, it was as if something had been pulled out from inside me. I felt like something has been broken in my heart, and I was free from it. I continuously repented from the past, which the Lord has shown me.

After two months, I felt like I went through a course of healing and repentance. I was free.

This feeling or experience is impossible to describe with words. I was like a prisoner and now released and free. I knew God saved me from this bondage. The experience is unforgettable.

These memories still come to mind from time to time, but they have no authority or power within me. Their power is broken in my life. They no longer control me.

And then I asked God what to do next. And spoke a second time, saying:

"The fruits of being here with Me, you will see later..."

Then I knew it in my heart that I have to ask forgiveness from all the women I had used in my fornication. I tried to remember the names of all the women and made a list of them so I could find them and ask forgiveness and testify that I'm a new person and preach the gospel. I prayed for them and that God may guide me to find them. Some of them I did find some women I didn't. But I believe that God will lead me in time, and I'm always ready!

Ten years later, I was standing on the same hill with my pregnant wife and three children, thanking the Lord for their fruits.

INTRODUCTION

We live in a **sinful** world; this is a **fallen world**. This world doesn't belong to us anymore; it belongs to evil. We do not have to save the world; Jesus did not come to save the world, but **us** from it! We are not of the world **[John 15:19: John 17:14]**

> *"They are not of the world, just as I am not of the world"*
> *[John 17:16 ESV]*

He came to restore what was once taken, given: the relationship with true Lord God as it was in the beginning in the Eden. Jesus said **[John 14:6]**:

> "*I am the **way**, and **the truth**, and **the life** [or the one true way to have life]. **The only way to the Father is through me** [⌐ No one comes to the Father except through me].*

Why Jesus came? **The salvation of our souls** and to eliminate sin that prevents us from accessing our Heavenly Father's heart. It is essential to understand that today we already live **everlasting life**, the **life of eternity. The soul that we have is eternal;** however, the physical body dies – we call it "death", "*first* death". Unfortunately, we are so addicted to this world, and we don't want to understand and think about eternity. We like to live day after day and enjoy it. But this physical body is not as crucial as our soul. It has its **own purpose. This present life's decisions define how we spend eternal life,** whether we live with God and His Kingdom or whether we suffer torment in eternal fire, that is, the **second** death, known as *Hell*. As I said, the first death is "death of the body":

> *"Don't be afraid of people, who can kill the body but cannot kill the soul. The only one you should fear is the one who can destroy [*ᴸ both] the soul and the body in hell [*ᴸ Gehenna; 5:22].*" [Matthew 10:28]*

Our choices – what we sow is what we reap.
Sometimes people think that death is the easiest way to escape from current life to the unknown. But which is worse than death? Worse is **torture that never ends**; you suffer, and you can't die, and you burn with eternal fire. And you can't get out of it.

> *During those days people will look for a way to die [*ᴸ seek death], but they will not find it. They will ·want [long; desire] to die, but death will run away [flee] from them. [Revelation 9:6]*

Many among us do not even take it seriously and do not believe that *hell* exists. But we must remind ourselves that ***hell*** is not for people, but for the devil and Lord God doesn't want us to go there:

> *"Then the King will say to those on his left, 'Go away [Depart] from me. You will be punished [are cursed]. Go into the **fire that burns forever [eternal fire]** that **was prepared for the devil and his angels** [*ᶜ the demons]."* [Matthew 25:41]*

We have heard about it, but we have forgotten and do not understand its real meaning.
Why?
Because we have lost the **Fear of God,** and we have become **lukewarm [Revelation 3:16].**
We have conformed to this world [Romans 12:2], and we live

by sight, not in faith; and we walk by our **pleasures our flesh**: the **lust of the flesh** and **the lust of the eyes** and the **pride of life [1 John 2:16].** We have made our idols and our "**own** Jesus" **[2 Corinthians 11:4].** Completely different from the real Jesus Christ- **Jesus Christ, who will judge the world.**

To be honest, how we are different from the world?

We wear the "**mask of Christianity**": it means that we are "Christians" only on Sunday when we go to the church, but other days, we even behave worse than the world. We are such a two-sided and split personality: It's called "*identity crisis*".

We don't live by our words. I have been there for so many years, and **my biggest concern is losing faith among Christians. How many times have I doubted about my faith**? Again, too many times.

In these cases, *doubt* is good: doubts raise questions, and if our faith does not withstand trials, then that *faith* is not worth believing. We cannot bury our heads in the sand and ignore the questions; the *right* questions will come and they will not go away. No wonder we lose faith because **we do not dare to test our faith**.

---

*6 ·This makes you very happy [or Rejoice in this], even though now for a short time ·different kinds of troubles may make you sad [you have had to suffer various kinds of trials/testings]. 7 **These ·troubles [trials; testings] come ·to prove that your faith is pure** [to test and prove the authenticity of your faith; C a test that proves the genuineness of a valuable metal]. This ·**purity of faith [or tested and proven authenticity]** is ·**worth more** [more precious; more valuable] than **gold**, which can be ·**proved to be pure** [tested and proven authentic] by **fire** [Ps. 66:10; Prov. 17:3; 27:21; Zech. 13:9; Mal. 3:3] but ·**can [or will] be destroyed.** But the ·**purity [tested and proven authenticity] of your faith** will bring you praise and glory and honor ·when Jesus Christ is shown to you [L at the revelation of Jesus Christ]. 8 You **have not seen ·Christ** [L him], **but still you love him**. You cannot see him now, but you*

> believe in him. So you ·are filled [rejoice] with ·a joy that cannot be explained, a joy full of glory [an inexpressible and glorious joy]. ⁹ ·And **you are receiving [or ...because you are receiving] the ·goal** [outcome; purpose] **of your faith—the salvation of your souls. [1 Peter 1:7-10]**

Our attitude must be **fervent**, not **lukewarm**: "*to be or not to be*". But we are afraid that our faith will fail, because it's based on our ignorance and "*Christian bubble*".
Jesus **promised [Matthew 7:7-8; Luke 11:9-10]:**

> ⁷ ”·**Ask** [Keep asking], and ·God will give [ᴸ it will be given; ᶜ the passive verb implies God as subject] to you. ·**Search [Seek; Keep seeking],** and **you will find**. ·Knock [Keep knocking], and the door will open for you. ⁸ ·Yes, [ᴸ For; Because] **everyone** who asks will receive. **Everyone** who ·**searches [seeks]** will find. And everyone who knocks will have the door opened.

But answers don't come easily and by themselves; **you have to seek them! God reveals them who are passionate seekers.**

Another essential problem of losing faith among Christians is **unrealistic expectations:** that guarantee bitterness. It's because we don't read the bible and don't know the *real* God.
Keeping faith is also a spiritual warfare and **we must not give up**!

> ⁴ For **it is impossible to ·bring back again to a changed life [ᴸ renew again to repentance] those who were once ·in God's light [enlightened], and**
> ·**enjoyed** [experienced; ᴸ tasted] ·**heaven's gift** [or the heavenly gift; ᶜ perhaps the gift of salvation], **and ·shared in [partook of] the Holy Spirit. ⁵ They ·found out [ᴸ tasted] how good God's word is, and ·they received [ᴸ tasted] the ·powers [miracles] of ·his new world [the coming age/world]. ⁶ If they have ·fallen**

> *away [committed apostasy], it is impossible to ·bring them back to a changed life again [^L renew them again to repentance], because they are nailing the Son of God to a cross again and are ·shaming him in front of others [making a public disgrace/exhibition of him].*
> *[Hebrews 6:4-6]*

It means that we could lose our salvation! Many will lose faith [Matthew 24:10-13]:

> *¹⁰ At that time, **many will ·lose their faith [turn/fall away], and they will ·turn against [betray] each other and hate each other.** ¹¹ Many false prophets will ·come [appear; arise] and ·cause many people to believe lies [deceive many]. ¹² There will be more and more ·evil [sin; lawlessness] in the world, so ·most people will stop showing their love for each other [^L the love of many/most will grow cold]. ¹³ But **those people who ·keep their faith [endure; stand firm; persevere] until the end will be saved**.*

That *old* life that we have lived must end, and the only way to God is repentance through Jesus Christ.
It's the attitude of heart and the will and the decision that you really want change.
It starts with a longing, a longing for change. It begins with the fact that we are tired of being the same, and doing the same thing, waiting for different results.
I even may say that the *Faith* is not for the weak - it's for the strong ones.
The weak give up, the strong endure to the end.

The *TIME*
Nearly 150,000 people die **per day** worldwide, based on the latest comprehensive research published in 2017: these aren't *natural deaths*. Age is irrelevant.

16

We think that we have time and seems like the time is under our control.
But we really don't. It's one of the biggest deceptions, saying, "*I can still repent and make things right with God.*" NO! **Today** is the day! Not tomorrow or next week, **today**!

> "**Today** ·listen to what he says [*ᴸ* if you hear his voice…].
>   Do not ·be stubborn [*ᴸ* harden your hearts; Ps. 95:7–8]."
> **[Hebrews 4:7; 3:15]**

Your choice: Death or Life! [Deuteronomy 30:15, 19]

God sees **our motives and attitudes**; we cannot **deceive Him** in our **cunning** that I will come and think that He can't be "**exploited**."
We do not know how much time is given to us. We can say in our **pride** that "*nothing will happen to me*" or that "*I am already such a good Christian.*"
Besides, time is also individually **limited**: God's Grace and Mercy End: **The time for repentance is running out**; God still has patience, but **He will not allow himself to be mocked.**

> "*You remember that after Esau did this, he wanted to ·get [ᴸ inherit] his father's blessing, but ·his father refused [ᴸ he was rejected]. Esau **could find no way to ·change [or repent of]** what he had done, even though he ·wanted [pleaded for; sought] the blessing so much that he cried [Gen. 27:34–41].*"
> **[Hebrews 12:17]**

> *I have **given her time to change her heart and turn away from her sin** [repent of her sexual immorality], but she does not want to **change [repent]**. [Revelation 2:21]*

God hates the most when we play with His Grace!

We have heard so much about repentance and regret in the church and congregation, but we don't live it - we must do it, and at the same time, we feel an enormous burden of guilt that we are sinners. But we must not live under the burden of guilt, and we must understand that Jesus overcame the power of sin [Revelation 1:5]! We no longer have to be slaves to sin [Romans 8:2; Romans 6:22]

How many times have we "*repented*" and regret? I think that I have hundreds of times. What has changed? Nothing. Yes, I have **regretted** so much, but I still find myself doing the same thing again and again. Even **worse**, if I **promise** to myself, or swear to God, that I won't do this. Pretty soon, I find myself in a much difficult situation and doing it a hundred times worse things. Finally, I'm so tired of these situations, I want to change my life, but I can't. I don't have the strength to change my life; yes, I can change my habits by training and have some motivation from others, but it's not that. There's always something missing.
And I got news for you – You are not meant to fight alone, you can't raise yourself from your hair.
We need Jesus: whether we admit it to ourselves or not, that's the **truth**. Maybe it sounds already like *cliché*, but we need **real intervention**. I want **real Jesus**, not "*Jesus*" that our world has made.
Yes, we have **willpower**, but there are two sides to that; "*will*" and "*power*".
"*Will*" comes from us; "***Power***" comes from God.
That is not *true* **repentance**.

There's saying: **"***it's always **easier** said than **done**.*"**
But we make it harder. We complicate everything. Our **pride** makes it difficult.

There's a big difference between **regret, remorse,** and **repentance**, and we cannot confuse them.

If we _regret or have remorse_, it just shows that we have a conscience, but it doesn't change anything- the knowing. There is no _act_. Many will remain in remorse and regret; it will become **self-pity** and turns to **despair,** and despair brings forth death. But nothing will get better. It's just an **emotional stage.**
But **true repentance** is much more.

So, about _true_ **repentance**:

First (Humble): Regret and **remorse** are half of the repentance; that's why I talk about "**true**" repentance.
We sin against God **[Psalm 51:6],** so we have to repent of our actions.
Sin is very **specific.**
We can't **repent if we are not humble to God and admit our sin**. Only the humble heart brings repentance. Humbling yourself is the key because God is against the proud. And it's an **attitude of Heart**, knowing deep inside and **hoping** that **only** God can change you!

> _"Whoever makes **himself great** [lifts up/exalts himself] will be made **humble**. Whoever makes **himself humble** will be made **great** [exalted; lifted up]." **[Matthew 23:12; Luke 14:11]**_

> _" But God gives us even more grace, as ·the Scripture [⸠ it; or he] says,_
> _"**God ·is against [opposes; resists] the proud,**_
> _**but he gives grace to the humble** [Prov. 3:34; 1 Pet. 5:5]."_
> _**[James 4:6]**_

Second (Decision): Repentance is a **decision, changing heart** toward and **renewing our mindset** towards "_something_". This "_something_" is **sin,** but there are also some habits or some false thinking or attitudes that we have that are contrary to the nature of God and against His will. Everything is not sinning automatically.

It means: I will not do this again, I made my mind, that I don't want to do **this** anymore and you **turn 180°** and walk away from it and never look back. That's what Jesus teaches.

> Later, Jesus found the man at the Temple [area] and said to him, "See, you are well **now**. Stop **sinning** [*T* **Sin no more**] so that something worse does **not** happen to you." [*C* Sometimes, **not** always, suffering can be explained by **sin**.] **[John 5:14]**

Third (Price): But **we have to understand** that **repentance has a price tag**. What do I mean by that?
It means that this **decision** is a **matter of death and life**. It's the attitude of heart, knowing the price: if **I have to make a choice**: **"I'd rather die than go back to sin"**. That shows how much you really want to get rid of that sin and believe me, God sees when we are dead serious. That's the attitude of the heart! It literally means that you are ready to die for it. How many times I've heard that from people who have really repented? Too many! And they mean it, every word. That shows our **passion for God** that **we want Him** more than **sin**.

Fourth (Act):
If we make that decision, we have to stick with that. There's no going back. We can't reconsider, because we know the price. We need to keep going forward.
We need to **produce fruits**:
Like John said: **first repentance**, then baptizing with Holy Water and **then produce fruit [Matthew 3:8]**:

> **"Do the things [*L* Produce the fruit] that show you really have changed your hearts and lives [that prove your repentance; *L* of repentance]."**

The same thing said Paul **[Acts 26:20]**:

> *[Indeed; or On the contrary] I began telling people that they should **change their hearts** and **lives and turn to God** [repent] and **do things [works] to show they really had changed [L worthy of repentance].***

Churches and congregations don't talk about that. And there's a reason; how many could stay then? It's a **harsh truth.**

As I started this book with the testimony of Anre, that I have heard several times over the years, I finally understand the *true* **meaning of the repentance**. Without these *third* and *fourth* parts, there's no repentance because it's not final, and I know that I will fall. But what I did understand from Anre testimony, was that the **heart is** in all situations. The *true* **heart desperation** to God and understanding the **price** and staying and **producing the fruits of repentance** are the secrets.

And in that particular case, the **fruits** were that Anre started to search for forgiveness from these women, no matter what. We have to overcome shame and pride.

Fruits are that we **stay** in new repentance and become clean, whatever the sin was, we have renewed our mind and heart to never do it again. And make things right – if we stole, then pay back more than we stole; stop lying and confessing and ask forgiveness and speak the truth, etc. Some things can't be fixed, but **we can give our best, and God will to the rest.**

I know that's the hardest part to stay and produce fruits, but there's **a secret: You're not alone, He will not let you fall!**

WHY?

That **sin** would be revealed, and then it doesn't have authority.

> *"So **you must stop telling lies. Tell each other the truth** [L Let each one of you speak truthfully to his neighbor; Zech. 8:16], because we all belong to each other in the same body [L are members of one another]." [Ephesians 4:25]*

> *"[ᴸ Therefore,]* **Confess your sins to each other and pray for each other so God can heal you. When a believing person prays, great things happen** *[ᴸ The prayer of a righteous person is powerful and effective].* **" [James 5:16]**

Through repentance, we become a *strong* church and congregation and grow in *purity* to the *Body of Christ.*
There's a saying: **"a drop of tar in a honey pot spoils all the honey."** Through repentance, we become **Holy** and **Pure**.
So that we can **fight spiritual warfare** and to agree in the same mind in everything **[1 Corinthians 1:10]**:

> *I beg [urge; appeal to] you, brothers and sisters, by the name [or by the authority; or as followers] of our Lord Jesus Christ that all of* **you agree with each other** *and* **not be split into groups** *[divided into factions]. I beg that you be* **completely joined together** *[fully united; or made complete]* **by having the same kind of thinking** *[ᴸ mind]* **and the same purpose** *[intention; conviction].*

What makes me sad is that I also have seen that we know very little about **spiritual warfare** and **wisdom of God**; even the world knows better.

> **"My people will be** *[or are being]* **destroyed, because they have no** *[lack]* **knowledge. You have refused to learn** *[rejected knowledge; or failed to acknowledge me], so I will refuse to let you be [reject you as] priests to me. You have forgotten the teachings [law; ᶜ Hebrew: Torah] of your God, so I will forget your children." **[Hosea 4:6]**

Because we have **despised the wisdom of God and knowledge**, also, we have **worshipped the knowledge of the world.** But the world knows better about the spiritual world and its principles and laws than we Christians. This is a disgrace.

> "Yes, **worldly people** [ᴸ the children of this age] are more clever [shrewd; prudent] with their own kind [contemporaries; generation] than **spiritual people** [ᴸ the children of light] are."
> **[Luke 16:8]**

Thank Lord God for His grace, who has given us the Holy Spirit through the sacrifice of Jesus Christ – The Spirit, who is above all knowledge and miracles and wisdom. Before Jesus, the Holy Spirit wasn't available and free to everyone as a **gift**.

Can you even imagine if over **2.3** billion Christians (by statistics) were of the <u>same mind</u> and <u>agreed on the same thing</u>? Even **1%** of them? The world would be very different.

How many **will stand in faith** if Jesus comes? How many will be **deceived**?

> "**False Christs** [messiahs] and **false prophets** will come [appear; rise up] and **perform great wonders** [signs; miracles] and **miracles** [wonders; marvels]. They will **try to fool** [mislead; deceive] even the people **God has chosen** [elect], **if that is possible**." **[Matthew 24:24; Mark 13:22]**

That is why I wrote this book; so that we could prepare us as a church and **congregation** and the **Body of Christ**.
That is **practical Christianity**, and the **next chapter** talks about how to live it, **without any illustrations** in **actual life**.

This book also contains various and essential topics, *for example*:

Cheating
Love vs love
Fear vs fear
Debt
Good vs good
Slavery
(Homo)Sexuality
Adam and Eve
Money
Abortion
Friendship
Faith
Giving
Curse
Honor
Fornication
Sin

…and much more!

CHAPTER 1

Today **is the morning** when I made *"a step out"* from the current situation; I <u>literally</u> **crossed the line** that I **drew on the floor.**

As I **knelt** before the Lord God in my living room at 6 am, I **say**:

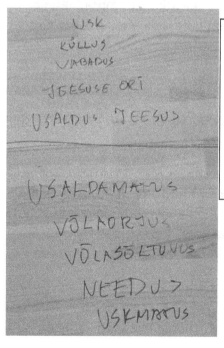

"Lord God, <u>destroy me before</u> I fall back to the **slavery of debt**! I rather die if I go back! That's enough for me! **Things have to change now!**
The presence and the power of the Holy Ghost fill and bear me!"

FAITH
ABUNDANCE
SLAVE OF JESUS
TRUST IN JESUS

UNTRUSTFUL
SLAVE OF DEBTS
ADDICTION OF DEBTS
CURSE
DISBELIEF

*This is how I started my morning prayer, and I'm so tired of this situation that has lasted over the year. I want Lord God more, and I give my **heart** and **soul** with all my mistakes and addictions to Jesus Christ, who already had died for me and resurrected from death that I could live forever!*
*"A Step Out" is also a physical activity; it is a declaration that now things are changing, and it has a deep meaning both in the spiritual world and in this because both worlds are interconnected, intertwined, bonded [**Matthew 16:19**].*
More than we could ever imagine.

From this day, I'm also in **payment default** – (Payment default is a violation of the debtor's monetary obligation for more than 45 days from the day following the due date and when the amount exceeds 30 euros)

*I am in a situation where I have **over-borrowed**, and at the same time, I have been unemployed for over a year and have not been able to pay the loan payments- there are reasons and explanations for everything…*

Repentance and a **new mindset** and **attitude of the heart** are badly needed! I also spoke in our men's brotherhood group about it. I believe that the release comes now! It is essential to understand why this happened. Where does the sin and curse come?
Why do I behave the way I do?

I have never been in such a bad situation! Only Lord God can redeem and make a miracle so that only He will be glorified!

CAN GOD GIVE ME THAT MONEY? I BELIEVE EVEN MORE!
[Ephesians 3:20]

God has shown that **MONEY AND DEBT SLAVE,** or the mentality/mindset, are both from my mother, who lives alone, has a good salary, but lives over her head, borrowing from her brother or mother. Of course, I understand that she has home loans. Also, my father, who lives by himself, has no dependents (the only son is already grown-up), uses the money unwisely, and borrows from his 77-year-old father. It has lasted for years.

> *It's not just my mother or father or me. – It's the world where we live in! That all world is based on addictions, deceive and manipulations. All the world is living in a debt bubble, and that's something new.*
>
> *Yes, we may say: "I'm earning money and I got to work and I can afford things to myself." But what do you actually spend your money on?*
>
> *This is the world of consumption, but if you borrow or take loan, that's problem from beginning! We don't know how to manage money, to collect, invest and manage money.*

BORROWING HAS TO STOP!

The same thing is with my grandmother (father's side); all the money that she inherited is wasted less than ten years.

> **"Stupidity is a curse, and God hates fools because they rebuke wisdom in Fear."**

> *Of course, now it's hindsight wisdom, but it's always about the state of mind, always reminds me of the parables of the "Bags of Gold /Talents" [Matthew 25:14-28].*

> **"SAVING A SOUL IS WORTH ANY PENNY!" [HP]**

"LODJAPUU" as our current living home is **one** of the reasons; in fact, it is a consequence of why we are in this situation. It belongs to my mother.
--It all started almost three years ago, when we lived in Tallinn, in a one-bedroom apartment with my four years old son and with my wife, being pregnant and waiting for the second son. So, we were looking for a bigger place to live, and we found a semi-detached house outside Tallinn, with three bedrooms. At the time, the real estate prices were very high, and we couldn't afford any houses in Tallinn, so that was a perfect solution at the time, but it was unfinished housing, but we had high hopes to finish it by ourselves- also, I **promised** it to my mother. All these real estate properties were my mother's because I'm unable to apply for a loan. Before that, we were willing to stay at the apartment, to avoid any deals with my mother, but she insisted, being worried about how could we manage in this small apartment. Basically, we changed one-bedroom apartment to three-bedroom semi-detached house one to one. Long story short. --
As the house was unfinished, the pressure of finishing was rising for two years, by my mother and also by my wife – I don't blame them, but we didn't have money to finish it. So, we "had to" take expensive loans to finish it, because the bank didn't lend us – the reason was that I had a payment default in 2017. Also, finished house is much easier to sell. We took loans several times, because we couldn't manage and finish the house.

What I've learned during this time? The biggest mistake was to make a **decision under pression of time,** because second child was already coming. But in the end, I'm very thankful to my mother.

These are just the reasons, not excuses – Of course, I admit that we also used money **unwisely** because of the situation that we live in. No doubt about it.

I'm the only one to **blame,** and I'm the only One who is **responsible.**

We tried to sell "LODJAPUU" twice in two years, in different ways. You, ABBA ELOHIM, will turn everything to blessings and winnings, to them, who love you! AMEN! **[Romans 8:28]**

Maila is spiritually breaking; I've noticed it very well today – I believe that our youngest son felt it when Maila burst into tears – Dear Holy Spirit, give us the strength and peace to our hearts and the taste of victory so that we could endure.

7 AUGUST

I prayed for parents - especially from my grandfather – because I have so much borrowed from him. It has to stop!

Grandfather "J" needs to get freedom and joy.
I talked to him yesterday. He complains that he couldn't figure out where the money is going; also, my father wants to get money from him to buy a car, and he borrows money every month. Also, grandma ran out of money and now have to carry her also.

> My father-side grandfather "J" has always been supportive; never judge over me, and my actions. He always supported me financially, and he never said, "NO." He always listened when I talked about my things and my relationships etc.

Today is the deadline to pay 350€ to the bank to avoid payment default and debt collector.
I don't have that money, but the Will of God may come, His solutions may come forward!

BUT I WILL NEVER BORROW THE MONEY from elsewhere.

At the end of the day, I was able to pay off because I received my unemployment money earlier.
It seems that Maila has started looking for solace elsewhere; in the evening, she began playing games with the tablet. I previously installed Mahjong to the tablet to play, even though I knew it was a stupid thing to do - so, Maila played two nights in a row until 1 am.

8 AUGUST — FIRST ATTACK

Tonight we experienced an interesting attack: In the middle of the night, our younger son "N "woke up in crying panic because he hit his head twice against my shoulder and couldn't fall asleep any longer.
Then Maila took him in her arms, and he pointed to my side of the bed and said "*ai-ai-ai,*" and he didn't want to go sleep, then I left the bed and went to another room to sleep.
Meanwhile, our older son "S" went to the bathroom and in the morning he told me he had a nightmare of me screaming and Maila strangling "N"
Attacks like this are coming, it's just a statement that we're on the right track,
and the enemy wants to kidnap our blessings and our freedom.

> *That's not common among us, such weird experiences- as I call them – "attacks"...These are echoed between the spirit world and the physical world; these two worlds are connected, bonded, more than we could ever imagine.* **[Matthew 16:19]**

9 AUGUST

My acquaintance "I" just called and asked me how I could bill him so he could pay for a website, that I made for his company. I wonder if guilt started and he asked how's my financial status is at the moment.

The Word of the Day: *"Keep working and success will come!"*

---

*Why am I referring to "acquaintance" not to a "friend?" Simple, not everybody we meet will become a **friend** right away; friendship is something that is **earned, proven** in times. It means that you're willing to give your life for him.*

> *„The **greatest love** a person can show is to **die for his friends** [*ᴸ No one has greater love than this: to lay down one's life for one's friends; ᶜ Jesus' **death is the ultimate expression of this principle**]." [John 15:13]*

*I have only a few friends whom I can count on, relay, trust, etc. That's enough for me! These things aren't **self-defined**.*

---

10 AUGUST

Lord God, please reveal to me about the **value of money**, that 1€ value will remain the same in **poverty** as in **wealth**.

11 AUGUST

Smoking - the war with the neighbor starts again (which has been going on over two years); I believe that is also one of the reasons why it is challenging to sell "LODJAPUU". If the buyer were a smoker, it would be super – little irony.

It's a *mental* struggle! Six times the smoke came into the room; I also sent an e-mail to the neighbor in the evening.

Dear Holy Spirit, it is a **spiritual** struggle, touch him and open his eyes! [Ephesians 6:12]

The most incredible thing is that he also smokes under his 2-year old daughter's nose while playing with her. If you don't care about other people, but what about our **own** daughter, flesh, and blood?

*From day one, we have a conflict with our neighbor over smoking because all the smoke comes through the ventilation and open windows into our rooms. We've talked to him about it several times. His first statement was that he wouldn't quit smoking because of us. Addictions blind people and make them in defense position like it's part of them. It's amazing. I've been in a similar situation before; my mother and father were smokers when I was a child, and I despise the smoke smell. Now, I have to be a secondhand smoker (passive smoker), especially my wife and two children. Emotionally, how could you react? Better question – how do you deal with this as a Christian? "Turn the other cheek" **[Matthew 5:39]** while he is killing your children slowly?*

My mother-in-law called Maila, and Maila **spread the gospel** to her mother so powerfully, even if the mother-in-law was drunk, she still started to think about **Hell** and **Heaven**.

My mother-in-law has been drunk for years; she always calls when she's drunk. We have spoken about alcoholism and addiction and spread the gospel so many times. But that's the ***Spiritual Warfare,*** *and we don't make compromises with evil, but we are always here if she needs us, and we will be supportive if it's needed. Lord God never despises and rejects a broken heart and Spirit!* ***[Psalm 51:17]***

One more thing – we have to remind ourselves that the *soul* isn't drunk, the *body* and *brain* are. It means: you can say something directly to the *soul,* and you may speak to the *flesh*: *"You shut up and obey, I'm not talking to you!"* And it works. ***Every word*** *that we* ***say*** *has a Power, and it will never return empty! [Isaiah 55:11]*

> *The same thing is true of the words ·I speak [ᴸ that go out of my mouth].*
> **They will not return to me empty.**
> *They make the things happen that I want to happen [accomplish what I desire/purpose],*
>   *and **they succeed** in doing what I send them to do.*

Never underestimate the power of words!

Why is that? Like my father said: "*A person is <u>most vulnerable</u> when he is **drunk** and when he is **asleep**!*" Because during this time, the <u>shield</u> is down. Our **consciousness** is weak or down. And I agree. For this reason, we must pray every night before going to bed for the **protection** of the blood of Jesus Christ, for our children and ourselves!

---

12 AUGUST   RENEWAL OF THE MIND

Jehovah's mercy and Christ's Love to my neighbor! The worst thing is that a person enjoys smoking and doesn't want to get rid of it! Please, Lord, open his eyes!!!

> *Some days ago, my older son "S" asked from neighbor: "Why are you smoking?" and he replied: "Because I love it"*
> *How fool man can be to say such things to a child? What example does it leave?*
> *Such foolish self-justification! If you don't have an answer, then don't answer or just admit that I have problem that I'm struggling, etc. Or if you don't admit, then think better answer and just analyze and ask the same question to yourself.*
> *It is not common sense!*

1€ - I have felt the value of the 1€: how much money is it. If you're poor and you don't even have the 1€, but if you have money, the more you get, the smaller 1€ becomes; the values are changing,

depending on your current bank account status.
The more money you have, the smaller and more meaningless 1
€, 10 €, 20 €, etc., becomes! That must change – **the attitude of
heart – renewal of the mind [Romans 12:2].**

Only the greedy know the "*value*" of the money, because they love
to own money, and they are money lovers – worship mammon
[1 Timothy 6:10]

Money *is an* **amplifier** *of* **heart attitudes** *and* **motives***!*

<table>
<tr><td>24 AUGUST</td><td>SECOND ATTACK</td></tr>
</table>

I've never experienced anything like this before:
I was suffocated at night, durable and long, and my throat burned.
Maila woke up and startled and told me to raise my hands! It could
have lasted a minute or more. Raising my hands helped a little bit,
and the air started to move, breathing recovered gradually within
five minutes.

In the morning, Maila said that she was calm, and the Spirit said
that I must raise my hands to free from suffocation. The idea, or
wisdom didn't come from her! Glory to Lord!

It was shocking that things happen so fast, after making **the
choice** of **Repentance**, but at the same time, the peace and joy
of the Holy Spirit are in me. On the contrary – I'm so excited
what's next; it only proves God Almighty existence!
"If there is a devil, there must be a God!"
*If evil makes a step towards me, I will make the leap towards
Lord God.*

You believe *·there is one God [or that God is one; Deut.
6:4]. ·Good [⊥ You do well]! But* **the demons believe that, too,
and they ·tremble with fear** *[shudder].* **[James 2:19]**

---

26 AUGUST

Need Revelation on these topics:

1.) Talent – many may think that talents are spiritual gifts in the parables that Jesus spoke **[Matthew 25:14-28]**. In different translations, these are referred to as *"talents"* and as *"bag of gold"* and it means money, gold literally.
2.) Who am I to you, **ABBA**? These are the questions that we struggle with every day.
3.) Love of Christ?
4.) What is the Step, the *"faith step"*?

There's something supernatural inside of me that carries me and doesn't allow depression to sink me - **Peace** and **Joy** beyond. **[Romans 14:17]**

---

*Don't forget that **Romans 14:17** "Peace" and "Joy" are emotional feelings, not a state of mind. Only the heart feels emotions like this. So, we can't just set aside our feelings, but they **can't define us**! Lord God gave us these, I also believe, those are gifts from the Lord. There's a secret – we have to find the balance between all, emotions, mind, heart, etc. That world is based on **feelings, emotions, and lust**.*

---

1 SEPTEMBER

Today I was able to talk to my grandmother "V" (mother-side) about God and death, **Heaven** and **Hell**, which has been challenging to do so far, and she hasn't accepted; she is already 87 years old. Surprisingly, she was relatively receptive.

> *My mother's relatives are Russians, my grandmother "V"*
> *basically was banished from Russia in the 1960s, and she*
> *married my grandfather "H". They had two children (boy and*
> *girl), but they divorced when the children were young. And since*
> *then, they have been enemies, accusing each other different*
> *things. My grandmother "V" still speaks of him and blames him*
> *all kinds of things – I'm not naive to believe everything because*
> *there's always two sides of the story, and I don't know the whole*
> *story, both parties, and it never interested me, until now…*
> *My compassion – all I see is bitterness, forgiveness, and*
> *disappointment.*
> *They are divorced over 40 years, and my grandmother "V"*
> *never got another man, she didn't move on in her life. That's the*
> *saddest part of the story.*
> *Everyone has his or her own story.*

2 SEPTEMBER   FASTING #1

The fasting begins, the last one to see miracles! I no longer have
the strength to continue, need answers! THE LAST STAND. Three
months in a row, I have fasted five days a month.

> *Fasting **must** have the **purpose** why I do it, and the expected*
> ***outcome**, the **answer**, **solution** – even the answer "no" is still*
> ***an answer**. If you seek Him, you will get an answer eventually.*
> *First, we have to **learn how to listen**. We have lost hearing with*
> *our **Ears of our Hearts**. We are addicted to the noise of the*
> *surroundings, from which we must separate ourselves.*
> ***[Matthew 6:6]***
> *We have such **high hopes** and **expectations** that Lord God*
> *should answer to us right away and the way we want, but first,*
> *we have to **be silent before** Him (be still) and **know** that He is*
> *the Lord God Almighty! **[Psalm 46:10]***
> *We are used to getting everything quickly and according to our*
> *will, but its deception – such a **mindset produces only***

> *disappointment.*
> <u>*We lack patience.*</u>

Tomorrow on the 3 September and 5 September, I will receive payment defaults.

1.) What do I feel?
That I have been deceived, I am like a crazy religious, panic, sadness, etc.

2.) What do I believe?
I believe that breakthrough is now! There's nowhere to go, no turning back.
***Jesus** is the **only salvation**!*

3.) Where do I have to go?
I no longer know what to do, Faith does not grow, but hope decreases.

BUT there is something inside me… I can feel it with my whole body, soul, Heart, Spirit. There is something BIG and POWER… I can't explain – That "*thing*"-
He won't let me get buried in depression, start panicking, and drinking, etc.

GOD DOES NOT TORTURE!

The day before yesterday, 31 August, Maila and I began to discuss in the car about people's agreements, whatever they make.

> *It was just a discussion about agreements people are making, example: investments in their business; some random agreements which has a monetary value; agreements or contracts with guarantees (some real estate, deposit, etc.) Or some "innocent" agreements, etc.*

We came to the brief conclusion: **When money is involved, there is always a curse waiting to unleashed if the agreements are not fulfilled.**
The important thing is that if there are different parties and I am a third party, and if I made an agreement with one party, then it is also true in the spiritual world!
And if I break this agreement, even if I am an accomplice, I am also responsible! That's how it works in this world! I have seen it so many times in people's life's.

We need Jehovah's Grace!
Jehovah is Righteous; **we are not**!

---

*We **must seek** the **Righteousness of God** with our hearts because He is Righteous! That is part of His character.*

[Matthew 6:33]
*It's not **our** righteousness that we demand. Everybody demands his or her **own** justice, but Lord God's righteousness is all over the earth. Even you and me will be judged righteously.*

*Now I like to throw a line and make difference between the word "**judge**" and "**rebuke / exhort / reprove / admonish**", because I very often see, that we don't make differences between them and where we could use them. I see so many times, if one brother in Christ wants to rebuke or exhort, etc. other person, friend, acquaintance – then the that person accuses brother in Christ judging over him/her. Same thing I've seen in church, with fellow brothers or sisters in Christ.*
Of course, it's just self-defense and sometimes it may be justified, it depends on the attitude of first party and the situations. But 90% it's just self-defense of our pride to protect our reputation and ignore the problems.
*We have to understand that it all are based on **Agape's Love**, which is the **second most important commandment:***

> „And the second command is like the first: 'Love your neighbor as you love yourself [Lev. 19:18].' „ **[Matthew 22:39]**

We have to grow in Agape's love, but that's not an **excuse** to **let all behave like they want**, and **do what they want in the Body of Christ** – in the church and in the congregations! And that "Agape's Love" is often abused as a defense: "You must love me as I am!" It's a selfish – yes, Lord God will take **as you are**, but He will **never stay the same**!

**First**, let's talk about what we as Christians **must have**:
We have to own our opinion, and we are afraid to speak about it because others will take it as a judgment, so we are "spineless "Christians, fearful of what people say or do. We need to make our voices loud that we do not agree and stand what is **God's Righteous** and demand it!

And now what Christian **must do:**
We must rebuke, exhort, reprove, admonish and **warn like Paul and Jesus** did and others in the bible.
There's also a "**but**" in these topic, we will get to it soon.

To **warn** Christians and the world, needs the most courage! But we must do it - It's our duty!

> **But if you warn the wicked and they do not turn from their wickedness or their evil ways [wicked lifestyle], they will die because of their sin. But you will have saved your life [soul]. [Ezekiel 3:19]**

> **But if you warn the wicked to stop doing evil [turn from their ways] and they do not stop, they will die because they were sinners [for their iniquity]. But you have saved your life. [Ezekiel 33:9]**

> **But if you have warned those good people [the righteous] not to sin, and they do not sin, they will surely live, because they believed [took; received] the warning. And you will have saved your life [soul]." [Ezekiel 3:21]**

*Secondly, we have to understand that we, as Christians, **must not judge over the world**, over the people who are **in the world. [Matthew 7:1-2]:***

> *"Don't **judge** others, or you will [so that you will not] be judged. ² You will be **judged** in the **same way that you judge others**, and the amount you give to others will be given to you [or the standard you use for others will be the standard used for you; ᴸ with the measure you measure, it will be measured to you].*

*It's one of the **Spiritual laws**, if you judge, you will be judged; but if you forgive, you will be forgiven! **[Luke 6:37]**:*

> *"Don't judge others, and you will not be judged. Don't **accuse others of being guilty [condemn others]**, and you will not be accused of being guilty [condemned]. Forgive [Pardon; Release], and you will be forgiven [pardoned; released].*

Judgment's punishment was death; that was the measure in ancient times.

*There's also an **exception:***
We as Christians are allowed to judge in the church, congregation, so that the Body of Christ would be pure! That is our job to cleanse [1 Corinthians 5:7] the Body of Christ: *congregation/church.*

> *It is not my business to **judge those who <u>are not part of the church</u>** ᴸ outside]. **God will judge them.** But you **must***

> judge the people who are <u>part of the church</u> [*L* inside]. The
> Scripture says, "**You must get rid of** [expel; remove] **the**
> **evil person among you** [Deut. 17:7; 19:19; 22:21, 24; 24:7]."
> [**1 Corinthians 5:12-13**]

In the same scripture, Paul **rebuked** Corinthians church for in
its **wickedness. Wickedness** what heard to be much worse
than among **pagans, gentiles [1 Corinthians 5:1]**
Even more, Paul **rebuked** and said **[1 Corinthians 5:11]:**

> I am writing to tell you that **you must not associate with**
> **those who call themselves ·believers in Christ [a brother**
> **or sister] but who sin sexually**, or are **greedy**, or **worship**
> **idols**, or ·**abuse others with words** [slander], or **get drunk**,
> or ·**cheat** [swindle] people. Do not even eat with people like
> that.

Paul did not take this matter lightly, on the contrary, he
condemned it!
Do we still think, that things has got better in few thousand
years? No, much worse!
There's saying: "As strong as the church is, so strong is the
country"

Jesus spoke about **overall, general judgment, and the**
principles of the spiritual law, but Paul spoke about
exception about the Church– there are **no contradiction!**

Do not make compromises with evil! He / She will get the time
and opportunity to repent and ask forgiveness, but it doesn't last
forever! But we are so afraid of throwing people out of the
church:

> "Our bragging [boasting] is not good. You know the saying,
> "Just a little yeast [or leaven; *C* leaven is a small lump of
> fermented dough used to make a loaf rise, as yeast is

> *today]* **makes the whole batch of dough rise [^C yeast/leaven symbolizes the permeating influence of this man's sin within the community; <u>Gal. 5:9</u>." ^7 <u>Take out all [Cleanse; Purge] the old yeast [leaven] so that you will be a new batch of dough without yeast [leaven], which you really are "[1 Corinthians 5:6-7]</u>**

Thirdly, the word "**but**" that I mentioned before, which is the foundation and most important.

We like to quote what Jesus **exhorted**: **[Matthew 7:3-4; Luke 6:41-42]**

> "Why do you notice the **little piece of dust [speck**; *tiny splinter]* in your friend's *[^L brother's (or sister's)]* eye, but you don't notice *[consider]* the ·big piece of wood *[log; plank; beam]* in your own eye? ^4 *How can you say to your* ·friend *[^L brother]*, 'Let me take that ·**little piece of dust [speck**; *splinter] out of your eye'*? Look at yourself *[^T Behold]*! **You still have that big piece of wood** *[log; plank; beam]* **in your own eye.**

But why don't we read on? **[Matthew 7:5; Luke 6:43]**:

> "You hypocrite! **First**, **take the ·wood** *[log; plank; beam]* **out of your own eye. Then you will see clearly to take the ·dust [speck; splinter] out of your** ·**friend's** *[^L brother's]* **eye.**"

So, the "**but**" is that we must be **pure** and **clean** from the exact sin, that we see in others.
We must be repented and be example to others.
Then we have **right** to **rebuke, exhort,** etc. so that evil could not accuse us in the same.
To clarify: I have to deal with my problem (sin), the same problem (sin), and if I'm done, then I can tell my brother about

the issue or the sin that he has! It's giving the right name for the issue or the sin so that he could repent, and we could win this together if needed! And if he doesn't want to repent (everybody have time for repentance, but it's limited), then <u>deliver this man to Satan</u> for the destruction of the flesh, <u>so that the spirit may be saved:</u>

„**then hand this man over to Satan.** So **his ·sinful self will be destroyed** [sinful nature will be purged; or body/flesh will be destroyed; or body will be beaten down by sin], and **his spirit will be saved on the day of the Lord.**" **[1 Corinthians 5:5]**

Even Jesus **encouraged** us what we have to do **[Matthew 18:15-17]:**

"If your ·**fellow believer** [ᴸ brother (or sister)] **sins against you,**[a] go and tell him **what he did wrong** [ᴸ reprove/convict/correct him] in **private** [ᴸ between you and him alone]. If he listens to you, you have **helped that person to be your brother or sister again** [ᴸ gained/won back your brother (or sister)]. ¹⁶ But if he refuses to listen, **go to him again and take one or two other people with you.** '**Every case** [matter; charge] **may be proved by** [the testimony of; ᴸ the mouth of] **two or three witnesses'** [Deut. 19:15]. ¹⁷ If **he refuses** to listen to them, tell **the church. If he refuses to listen** <u>to the church</u>, then <u>treat him like a person who</u> **does not believe in God** [pagan; Gentile] or like a tax collector.

We have to **grow** in **Holiness and become one (Agape love is part of that)!**
"**Holy**" - means being right with God, who walks with God and within whom dwells the Holy Spirit.
We like to make things complicated and we have lost the true meanings of words, and we like to interpreted like world does.

So, we have to be ready, doesn't matter, if we like it or not:

„*Preach the Good News [Gospel].* **Be ready at all times** *[whether it is* **convenient** *or* **inconvenient**; *in season or out of season], and tell people what they need to do [correct; reprove].* *Tell them when they are* **wrong [Rebuke]**. *Encourage [Comfort; Exhort] them with* **great patience** *and* **careful teaching** *[L all patience and teaching],"* **[2 Timothy 4:2]**

"*Finally then, brothers, we ask you, and* **exhort** *in the Lord Jesus that just as you received from us how you ought-to be* **walking** *and* **pleasing** *God (just as you also are walking), that you be abounding more."* **[1 Thessalonians 4:1 DLNT]**

Conclusion; *to make things even easier and clear, there are three stages (we're still talking about Body of Christ):*
*1.) Be right with God (**Holy**) without sin*
2.) Rebuke / exhort, etc.
3.) If second doesn't give result and they don't repent, then we judge and throw out!

In churches and congregations, there are so many rich people, whom we are afraid to **rebuke / exhort**, *because they bring* **money** *and* **fame** *to church / congregation!*
But we shouldn't. And let the Holy Spirit give us boldness!

„*[L For] Our* ·**appeal** *[encouragement; exhortation]* **does not come from** ·**lies** *[error] or* ·**wrong reasons** *[false motives; L impurity], nor* ·*were we trying to* **trick you** *[with guile/deceit].* ⁴ *But we speak the* ·*Good News [Gospel] because God* ·*tested [approved] us and* ·*trusted us to do [or entrusted us with] it. When we speak,* **we are not trying to please people**, *but* **God**, *who* ·*tests [examines; approves] our* **hearts**. ⁵ *You know that we* never ·tried to influence you by saying nice things about you [*L* came with words of flattery]. ·We were not trying to get your money; we had no selfishness to hide from you [*L* ...nor with hidden motives of greed]. God ·knows that this is true [*L* is (our) witness]. **6 We were not looking for human ·praise [glory], from you or anyone else," [1 Thessalonians 2:3-7]**

Who will purify Body of Christ?

We do! It's our mission and we are responsible for that!

„Since we have these promises, beloved, **let us cleanse ourselves from every defilement of body and spirit, bringing holiness to completion in the fear of God."[2 Corinthians 7:1 ESV]**

There's **only one** Body of Christ with many members, **not multiple bodies [1 Corinthians 12:13; Romans 12:5; Colossians 1:24]:**

"For just as the body is one and has many members, and all the members of the body, though many, are one body, so it is with Christ." **[1 Corinthians 12:12]**

But if one suffers, all suffer and on the contrary.

"If one member suffers, all suffer together; if one member is honored, all rejoice together." **[1 Corinthians 12:26 ESV]**

Yes, we as Body of Christ have many **functions** and we are depended each other.

"For as in one body we have many members, and the members do not all have the same function," **[Romans 12:4 ESV]**

"The eye cannot say to the hand, "I don't need you!" And the head cannot say to the foot, "I don't need you!" 22 ·No! [ᴸ On the contrary,] Those **parts of the body that seem to be the weaker are ·really necessary** [essential; indispensable]. 23 And the **parts of the body we think are less ·deserving** [honorable] are the **parts to which we give ·the most** [special; greater] **honor.** We ·give special respect to [or treat with special modesty] **the parts ·we want to hide** [that are shameful/unpresentable]. 24 The more ·**respectable** [presentable] **parts of our body need no special care.** But God put the body together and gave ·more [special] honor to the parts that need it 25 so ·**our body would not be divided** [or there would be no division in the body]. God wanted the **different parts to care the same for each other.**" [1 Corinthians 12:21-25]

Still we have to intervene, not make faces like it's none of our business! No, **we stand** for the **Body of Christ as a whole, not just our toes or fingers.**

There's no difference how many Christian churches or congregations we have, we all are the same in on **Body**.
And we have a helper **[John 14:26],** Holy Spirit, who unites us as one!
We stand for the **Body of Christ as a whole, not just our toes or fingers.**

Maybe you ask:" What do you mean by "toes and fingers"?"
Paul said that there are many different **Gifts of the Holy Spirit**, which we are **called** to **serve each other**, in the **Body of Christ.**
Not everybody are called to be teachers, not all them are. We have to discover, and grow by practicing in our **gifts in the church, congregation!** There's about **16 different Gifts of the**

Holy Spirit [Romans 12:6-8; 1 Corinthians 12:8–10]

> „Anyone who speaks should speak ·words from God *[or oracles from God; or as one bringing God's message]*. Anyone who serves should serve with the strength God gives so that in everything God will be ·praised *[glorified]* through Jesus Christ. **Glory** and **power belong to him forever and ever** [Col. 3:17]. **Amen."** [1 Peter 4:11]

At the end: I'm not talking about to shame us all, but like Paul said:

> *"I am not writing this to make you feel* **ashamed***, but to* **warn** *[admonish; correct] you as my own dear [beloved] children."* *[1 Corinthians 4:14]*

And this is why I needed to speak about that topic that is so essential in the church, congregations:

> *"Now I* **exhort** *you, brothers, by the name of our Lord Jesus Christ, that you all be speaking the* **same thing***, and that there* **not be divisions** *among you, but that* **you be made-complete in the same mind and in the same purpose***." [1 Corinthians 1:10 DLNT]*

Jesus never made compromises, never ran after anyone, etc. *Neither did Paul. Paul was full of* **humbleness** *and* **Agape Love** *and, at the same time, very* **specific** *and* **straightforward** *that even people wanted to throw stones at him. I say this, once more, seriously: we need to remove sin among us and start to clean the Body of Christ as a congregation and church, by* **starting with repentance***.*

Don't leave me and my **hope** and my **Faith** in **shame!**
[Psalm 25:3; Romans 10:11; Isaiah 28:16; 1 Peter 2:6]

Please give me a **new** and **pure heart** that is pleasing to you,
YHWH, not deceitful and protected from the evil of the Blood of
Jesus, from the deceptions of bitterness, pride, and on the tables
of the heart written Jehovah's Reverence, humility, Jehovah's
truth, righteousness, and **justice**!!!

A heart, that is full of Jehovah's **wisdom** and **courage,**
obedience, and **faithfulness**!

> There's also **hidden secret** behind the slogan **"pure Heart":**
> **You will see God!** - And that's a promise from Jesus himself
>
> > „They are blessed ·**whose thoughts are pure** [or whose
> > hearts are pure; ᵀ the pure in heart],
> >   for **they will see God."** [Matthew 5:8]
>
> It's not **an allegory or rhetoric or parable** – this is **real!**
> That isn't something impossible to achieve, "pure heart "is that
> you pour everything out to God, your thoughts, your feelings -
> doesn't matter how ruined and perverted these are – who do we
> fool? Lord God knows everything already, but He wants you to
> be sincere, openhearted. It's the same as a child and his
> Father, Father already knows, what a child has done, but
> sharing your heart is the key. He wants the real relationship,
> with flaws, with mistakes and all – so He could make you
> complete, perfect!
>
> > „So [Therefore] **you must** be **perfect**, just as your
> > Father in heaven is **perfect."** [Matthew 5:48]
>
> Yes, you can **become** perfect! **Lord God is perfect**, and He will
> never leave you broken and imperfect (Our understanding of

being "perfect" or "holy" is corrupted by the world view).
We have to have a **passion for the Heart** of **ABBA** ("Father" in Jewish), the Lord God. The **desire** for ABBA's Heart has to come from our own heart!

---

6 SEPTEMBER   **FASTING #5**

God is **GOOD**!

Only Lord God is **GOOD**! There's nobody else who is **Good**. These are Jesus' words, not mine **[Mark 10:18; Luke 18:18]**! Yes, we can do good things and do good for others, but it doesn't mean we are good; our motives define our actions. We have to be honest with ourselves, why we do what we do – is to get attention, ambition, praise, glory, to like people, some satisfaction of our ego? – Don't let us be deceived by it! Jesus also rebuked us:

Be careful! When you do good things, don't do them **[or Be careful not to do/parade your righteous deeds]** in front of people to be ·seen [noticed] by them. If you do that, you will ·have no [lose the] reward from your Father in heaven. 2 "[L So] When you give to the poor, **don't be like the hypocrites. They blow trumpets [C either figuratively ("blow their own horn")** or literally, since trumpets sometimes announced public events] in the synagogues and on the streets so **that people will see them and ·honor [admire] them**.
I tell you the truth, **those hypocrites** already have their full reward [C praise from people, rather than reward from God]. 3 So when you give to the poor, **don't let ·anyone know what you are [L your left hand know what your right hand is] doing**. 4 Your giving should be done in ·secret [private]. Your Father can see what is done in ·secret [private], and he will reward you. **[Matthew 6:1-4]**

I **decided** that Jesus is my Savior!

49

I pray for **Faith**, even the size of a mustard seed, to tell one million € to come here!

I threw away the shirts from my previous job, slicing them pieces and removed logos.

It's been in my heart for some time now – not to wear meaningful *symbols* and s*igns* knowingly.

In my case, I felt that something is still unfinished and holds me back; we will see eventually.

> *Signs and symbols have meanings, and by wearing them, you will be influenced by it.*
> *It's the same question again, why do we wear these things – motives – take for an example, any well-known brand– it is a sign of wealth, fashion presents so much impurity and lust, etc. Same with rings, it indicates being part of some agreement, some family, some commitment, Authority, spiritual, etc. A wedding ring presents a union between the man, the woman, and God. We forget that the marriage alliance has the third party of the covenant - Lord God.*

UNITY

We need to become as one with Maila! In all things! Pray together daily; never miss praying.

We have started praying together two times a day.

> *"Unity" – between **husband** and **wife**; the way Lord God made us. That is the Union above every other union in this world, and the devil knows that. He struggles to destroy it in every means necessary. That is what's going on today, so many Christians divorce their long marriages; the percentage of divorces among Christians is higher than non-Christians, and it is a disgrace. Our union is meant to be the strongest. There are so many reasons, but the source is still the same - our egos, our pride,*

*and laziness: **lack of humbleness.***
In the years we conform to the world,

> *„**Do not be ·shaped by** [conformed to; pressed into a mold by] **this ·world** [age]; instead be **·changed within** [transformed] by ·a **new way of thinking** [or changing the way you think; ᴸ the renewing of your mind]. Then you will be able to ·decide [discern; test and approve] what ·God wants for you [is God's will]; you will know what is good and pleasing to him and what is perfect"* **[Romans 12:2]**

*and take marriage for **granted**, and we don't strive for our relationships.*

*The **relationship is like a fireplace**; if you want the fire to burn, you have to add more wood continuously; otherwise, it will fade, and in the end, it dies.*
*Go back to your **first love**; remember the feeling of being in love.*
Most important**: doesn't matter, what you feel, the union is not about what you feel, is **a covenant**, **decision** that you made in the beginning. And the covenant is signed by the Lord God. It means you have a helper, but you still have a **free will.
*Husband and wife are made to become as **ONE [Ephesians 5:31; Matthew 19:5; Mark 10:8]***
*We have to get a revelation about what "**Unity**" truly means!*
Unity is based on love!

At the end of fasting – don't be disappointed if you don't see any changes, didn't get your answers; don't limit the Lord God, just wait.
Commonly, we don't get answers to what we **want**, but we will get answers that we **need** even if we didn't know the question or didn't ask it.

Also; It doesn't mean if you don't see the changes that there aren't any, our eyes are limited and blinded, so it doesn't mean that nothing changed in the **spiritual world**!

Fasting isn't twisting God's hands to get your will; no, <u>it is the humiliation of your soul and Heart so God could take you seriously</u>.

<u>Humbleness is the way to ABBA's Heart</u> *[Matthew 23:12; Luke 14:11; Luke 18:14]*

A good example is Daniel **[Daniels 10:12]** when he prayed and fasted for his people, and an angel Gabriel came and said that Daniel's words were heard <u>from day one</u>, and immediately, resistance broke loose in the spirit world.

So, don't underestimate and revoke your fasting with your words and disappointment!

7 SEPTEMBER   **DREAM and ATTACK**

Maila and I started the morning with prayer.

<u>Last night I had a **spiritual** and **powerful dream**</u>:

"I saw an Angel, and he gave me a small wooden sword. At first, it seemed to be an ordinary old wooden sword, but in the presence of demons and enemies, it resized and burst into flames. Then I realized that it is a **Spirit Sword**.

Then the enemy said: "**You will regret, Son of Ruach Ha-Kodesh**!" and then he fled.

It all happened after some kind of battle. Also, I remember that the Angel was a mighty warrior Angel, and when he gave me the sword, he spoke **words of blessings**.

I couldn't hear these words precisely because it was an out-of-my-body experience, and I saw myself drifting away; it all happened in some kind of an abandoned church.

These words of blessings were not in a recognizable language; I believe these words were in the **language of Angels**."

> *"**Son of Ruach Ha-Kodesh**" (means the Holy Spirit; the Holy Ghost): just struck me so profoundly, and these words started to echo.*
> *I still wonder, why didn't I hear these words, but I believe that in time, it will reveal me, at the very moment when I need them most. These words aren't lost; these words are still in me!*

Honestly, I had never seen spiritual dreams, before the year 2015 *(definitely not visions, I hope that I'm not exaggerating, at least I don't remember any)* when I started to seek the Lord God **truly** and **fervently**. [Matthew 6:33]

Immediately in the morning, my father began to draw parallels in the blessings of Pat Robertson and me, implying that I'm walking in the curse, and then asked me which of us is blessed; Pat, who has $100 million or me, who had lived his whole life in debt.

> *Yes, it's true - when I was about 16 years old, the Holy Spirit spoke to me about money and said: "**I will make your biggest weakness, be your strength, and many will be blessed through it**."*
> *There's always a <u>price tag</u>; nothing comes cheap. To get something, you have to give something. I've never been greedy or money-lover, and I know that I never will be.*
> *Owning money gave me satisfaction to buy things that made me happy, there was an empty hole in me, and I believe that is related to my "**father's love**" that I didn't receive. There are so many things related to lacking the "**father's love**."*
> *That emptiness will follow us through our entire life if we don't understand that there's only one "Father's Love," and it's from the Lord God as ABBA.*
> *Jesus was the expression of **ABBA's Love** (**true** Father's love), "**Agape Love**."*
> *This "**Agape Love**" is all we need, and <u>Jesus is the **only** way</u>.*
> *(Why not „mother's love"? New Testament doesn't refer much to*

53

> „mother's love", because „**it's elementary**" and "mother's love"
> isn't discriminated)

Attacks like this from my father are painful and very emotional, especially when I'm unemployed the second time, and I'm in debt.

There's something between us; we both have something.
EXPOSE NOW!

Yesterday, we talked about our mistakes and how we have missed the target. Father has never admitted his failures.

What's going on in his **heart**?

8 SEPTEMBER   TESTIMONY

I pray for grace and mercy that Lord God would show me, what is that is between us and what's bothering him; I don't see any changes in his behavior; he swears more, speaks filth, and is more nervous.

Does my being unemployed affect him so much?

What is **the Faith**? Abraham had Faith; he just believed!
He didn't perform any miracles, write beautiful songs or psalms, didn't kill any lions or Goliath.
What is the mustard seed?
Lord God's salvation is **perfect**!

Maila confessed that until today, she felt that she **must** pray when I reminded her in the evening that we have to pray. She took praying as an **obligation**, but now she **decided** that she **wants** to pray!

Today, in our fellowship group, we talked about the *true*
Repentance that Christians have not done so far.

**Half or *unfinished* Repentance brings disappointment in God
because we don't receive healings and freedom!**

> *How many times have I told Lord God and myself that I will
> never do this again? I even promised God, and myself but late
> on, I still found myself doing it and breaking my promises, and
> the situation is worse than ever. That's where the phrase **"never
> say never"** came from. Therefore, **we are afraid to say and
> promise something.***

It's Wednesday, and I have to be paid 720€ (from
1157€) for the evening to the builder "S."

Loaning is not even an option, from debt to debt.
Let the will of God to be born!
The mindset must be *creative, developing, operating,* and
masterful, not being in *debt,* and lend money and live beyond your
ability.

> *As I mentioned before, we tried different ideas to sell our
> unfinished house. In the end, we borrowed money to finish
> some works; for example, construction man installed street
> stones in our yard and some other works to make the house
> easier to sell. But still, I ran out of money, and I owe him money.
> We had over 15 interested people during the month, but for
> some reason, they just disappeared. Our plan was the sell the
> house, so we could pay back debt and build a smaller home*

---

without a loan. At the time, real estate prices were high, and demand exceeded expectations.

A mindset of debt slavery – *I believe that* **debt is a curse,** *and* **borrowers are slaves to lenders [Proverbs 22:7]**
Being in debt or on the way there, because of borrowing and couldn't pay back anymore – is a journey, it doesn't happen overnight: You just need or want the money and thinking that in one day I can pay. After a few times, you start to ignore the current situation, not consciously, it just blinds you, and it has power over you, and you have lost control, even if you know that you're doing is wrong. Precisely the same thing as with smokers. Warnings are written on the cigar package, you know them, but you don't understand, or you just don't get it. Then you just give up and don't care anymore, because if you look back, it's terrifying and you think that there's no turning back. Your bright mind says one thing, but your acts are different. You don't have to be a rocket scientist to understand that you're in debt. Despair and depression has you.

---

12 SEPTEMBER

Maila is **emotionally broken**, and she wants to take a loan.
She said, "**now I know how you felt all this time.**"

ABBA, help!

The pressure is rising every day, and now is the breaking point.

Our **own** race:
I don't want to give up five meters before finishing if 55 kilometers is already behind.
This is the race that is set before us to finish it **[Hebrews 12:1].**

We don't race with others, no, only by ourselves – that's the spiritual race.

I'm crazy, and I believe that Jesus saves! There's nothing impossible.

> *The bible is full of extraordinary miracles. I just don't want them to be only in the bible and stay there;* **Jesus is the same yesterday and today and forever. [Hebrews 13:8]**
> *So I* **believe** *that miracles are still possible in the 21st century, today, even greater miracles* **[John 14:12]!**

13 SEPTEMBER

I've tried anything in my power and knowledge, tried different business ideas, but everything needs investments.
I don't gamble with others' money.

> *With people,* **money is never free**; *there are always strings attached, and you will always owe them, maybe not money, but in favors; you "helped" me, and now you* **must** *"help" me whenever I want - you are on a leash. That is the business and fallen world principles and benefits.*

Dear **Lord**, I know that you have everything, gold, money, and you are the only investor I need.
Please, give me some talents, so I could make it grow.
(Thinking like seeder.)

16 SEPTEMBER

Today I promised to builder "S" to pay off debt; I believed that the Lord God will make a miracle. He didn't come as we agreed.

Our fellowship meeting was canceled.

I've even tried online gambling; maybe this is one possible way, for just one time.

> *I am **very aware** that it's a very slippery way and addicting and seems fast and easy money, but it will swallow your life in a blink of an eye. How do we trust the Lord then? **Money doesn't grow on trees, or I don't have the privilege to own one.** I want to learn the ways of the Lord God, how He reacts, and what the solutions are – even if I fail big.*
>
> *We don't have to **afraid of failing**; yes, it has its price, but how do we learn then? From others mistakes? Usually, no, we need to understand, have a deep understanding, and know the meaning of the value. The same thing applies to the Passion of Christ, the purpose of the Cross, and the Resurrection. We need deep understanding, Revelation; it's not enough that somebody said: "Jesus died for you." Sometimes we have to fall in the bottom to understand the true meaning and break our ego during the process.*

17 SEPTEMBER

I went to "men's gathering morning," which takes place every Tuesday at 7 am, in Baptize Church on the other side of town. Today there were over 90 men who decided to wake up early and be a part of something greater.

I made a prayer request on paper (*1157€ or 1million €*), so nobody sees the request; the Pastor just puts his hands on a bucket full of requests, and all men pray together for this.

Also, I prayed loudly in front of all men that I could find a job.

After that, one Christian businessman came and said that I should go back to things that I can do. I answered that I don't know what my skills and specialty are.

Then he said, **"I don't seek gold from the soil, but I remove the soil to see the gold."**

Since today I got ill, 17-20 September.

18 SEPTEMBER

I got an offer today to speak on Youth Alpha in Kohila, and the subject is "Christianity." The date of Youth Alpha is 20 October. So, I took the offer.

21 SEPTEMBER

In the meantime, when I was sick, I understand that I have to talk to my uncle "M" (*mother-side*) about homosexuality. Becket Cook's testimony is proof that being **"gay" is not part of identity;** for his upcoming birthday, Becket's book is a perfect gift. I asked my mother to order the book.

Unfortunately, I haven't read the book yet, but I saw his video testimony.

> We need to be careful, and read first the whole story by ourselves, because there are **false testimonies** that at first seem to be right, but may lead ourselves to wrong path, and to self-justification as "gay-Christians" do.

Yesterday a builder "S" called, and I didn't answer because I was ashamed that I don't have the money. It has been over three weeks and no miracles from God either.

I know that I must face my fear and shame to talk to him honestly. It takes <u>courage to overcome fear,</u> shame, and cowardliness.

Come what may, but I won't seek to borrow money elsewhere!

I will humble my Heart before God, and I will stand in Faith!

Last night, three times in an hour, smoke came into our bedroom,

and wow, how angry I got. I must talk to him about this again.
I pray for Lord God's wisdom and the Holy Spirit's words to speak.

22 SEPTEMBER

Yesterday I talked to the builder "S" about our situation and said that I would pay my debt, and I am responsible for my actions. It was amazing that he wasn't judgmental and angry. Every thought and fear I had concerning talking to him was gone. Like they say, **"fear has big eyes"**.

The miracle that we prayed with Maila, never came.
But I believe that the Lord God saw my heart and my courage to take responsibility and humble myself.
I believe it's just a beginning! It was a test to see if I would break or not, mentally.

Maila and I have prayed continually, being on the same in mind, twice a day.

> *Jesus said to the disciples:*
>> *"Truly I tell you, **whatever** you bind on earth will be bound in heaven, and **whatever** you loose on earth will be loosed in heaven."*
>> *"Again, truly I tell you that if two of you on earth agree about **anything** they **ask** for, it will be done for them by my Father in Heaven. For where two or three gathers in my name, there am I with them." **[Matthew 18:19]***

*It applies to all us who are children of God! Let it be according to your Faith! **[Matthew 8:13; Matthew 15:28]** We underestimate the Faith, let us not!*

23 SEPTEMBER

Questions of today:
What is Faith?
What is the measure of Faith for me? **[Romans 12:3]**

24 SEPTEMBER

I don't want to argue with my father – it's pointless and frustrating.
Tension with my father is because I'm still unemployed.

> *Arguing all the time makes the Holy Spirit sad; I even feel it with all my body. My blood is pumping, hands tremble, and it makes my heart sick. And that's the saddest part – I don't want to hurt Holy Spirit feelings and make him sad. [Ephesians 4:30]*
> *I need to find out what's wrong; I need to know these reasons*

25 SEPTEMBER

ABBA- what is the calling and **Your Will** for me?
I still haven't figured it out, why don't I hear you?
What is the door that you open for me?
I can't take it anymore... should I?
Where am I?

26 SEPTEMBER

Thoughts of the day:
*FAITH/DISBELIEF
*FEAR / SCARE
*COURAGE
*GOD'S WILL
*WORD OF JESUS

My uncle "M" bought an apartment near the sea, and then I
assisted him in moving from an old rental apartment to a new
single, and we had a disputation in the car about the cockroach as
if the Earth was millions of years previously. I also saw the
"homosexual spirit" of how it reveals itself, all those hand
gestures, and so on.

He is so convinced that we have evolved from apes, so I said
that's Darwinism is a proven myth a long time ago; it's only in
schoolbooks, which are century-old information.

> *Our family has talked to him about God years; he knows that we*
> *are Christians, and in some cases, he agrees with us. He is*
> *homosexual as long as I remember.*
>
> *In time, when you grow in the Lord, you will recognize the*
> *demons, and it makes you vomit spiritually.*
>
> *It doesn't matter if your homosexual or murderer or thief, child*
> *abuser, reaper, prostitute, "love of something," and so on* **[1**
> **Corinthians 6:9-11; Mark 7:20-23]; sin is sin, defilement is**
> **defilement.**
>
> *The main point is **that everything grows - all negative and all***
> ***the good things;***
>
> **Love grows; evil grows; _feelings_ grow, etc.**
>
> *I had a homosexual experience with my neighbor boy when I*
> *was about 6-8 years old.*
>
> *Children are so sensitive about all around us as they grow; also,*
> *their identity is growing, and they test everything if we let and*
> *favor and guide and give choices. We have spoiled and ruined*
> *our children from day one by liberty and choices. They are*
> *sensible and open to spirits, but we have to protect them! Then*
> *we are shocked when they are teenagers and don't **respect us,***
> *and their psyche is unstable and weak, and they are capable of*
> *all things. And what we do as parents? We don't take*
> *responsibility, and we blame society by denying that it was our*
> *fault.*

Of course, we try to take extreme measurements to deal with such kind of situations, but this doesn't work. And our world collapses.

I have only one question: where was a father? Why didn't he fulfill his purpose?

I remember so clearly when my father said that when I become a homosexual, he would shoot me. My family still doesn't have a clue.

*All feelings grow; it's just our **decision;** we will let them or not. It's a spiritual thing that attracts and pressures us and repeats all the time that **it's normal - it isn't; that's deception.***

*I know the **feeling**; <u>attractive; desire, adrenaline, heart rate rising, chicken skin, lustful,</u> etc.; first little bit terrifying in ignorance, but you get used to it. And later on, you already think it's normal, and part of you, part of your identity and you learn to defend it.*

I've felt this feeling, attraction a few more times, when I got older, about in the twenties.

*My thoughts were: I like that man, but I don't know why; there's something indescribable that drags toward him – but I know that I can't let it in, I can't give a space in my Heart **[Ephesians 4:27]** – I know that is a demon, who wants to pervert everything. There are so many reasons for this; secret feelings and secret sin **[Proverbs 28:13; Psalm 90:8]** – SIN grows!*

Eventually, there are no differences what you feel – the enemy is the same.

If you keep it secret, your secret sin will grow and takes root in your heart.

Most surprising is that most people acknowledge that they have a soul, but they don't understand that if there's a <u>soul</u>, then there must also be the <u>enemy of the soul.</u> It means that there's also another world.

It doesn't define my identity and me. The Jesus Christ defines me.

There's warfare against our "spiritual identity" and "gender

identity."

> *What is the purpose? The answer is simple: To destroy the relationship between a woman and a man and stop reproduction. Also, to lose our **soul**; so that we could reject Christ. Forgive me; I'm correcting myself: not "woman and man", but **"wife and husband"** because everything <u>outside the marriage</u> is **fornication**; doesn't matter how long have you been together or how many children do you have; **there's no covenant, and nothing binds you [John 4:17-18];** not even children these days!*
>
> *The only solution is Repentance; some repentances are easier to make, some not.*
>
> *For example, homosexuals (I don't refer to as "gay" because in the beginning, initially, it meant "cheerful." Same as with a "rainbow, "; they took a sign that was a covenant between the Lord God and man, and they just desecrated it and mocked.) Already think that it's part of their identity and it is an ongoing way of thinking, but it's constant life in sin.*
>
> *The same thing is with the verb "Religion" –the origin comes from Latin "**Religare**" means "**to bind; bond; obligation; reverence; to bind together."***
>
> *In one sentence: **"binding in unity with the Divine."** The motive was pure and noble.*
>
> *Evil always took something good, especially if it's from the Lord God and desecrates in any possible way.*

> **"The best deception that Satan has done is that he has made us believe that he does not exist."**

29 SEPTEMBER

Today, Maila and I got into a fight; she accused me of "blaming her" and "humiliating her" all the time – everything was about steaks she bought from the grocery; she didn't purchase exact steaks that I asked.

Because of it, she emotionally burst out all the feelings from inside and went to the bathroom to cry out and sat there for about an hour, and then she said she couldn't endure the situation any longer, to chase every 20 cents in grocery, etc.

Holy Spirit, please make me to better man and husband! Make me patient.

1 OCTOBER	REPENTANCE

All the debts will be transferred to a bailiff today, and contracts with the lenders will be terminated. That is what the enemy wants; for him, it's a victory.

I believe that God didn't allow us to give a loan to buy out *"LODJAPUU"* because I made a promise back in 2015, after selling our previous home "PEETRI" that I will never take a loan to buy a home and God wants **full deliverance.**

We're not buying out *"LODJAPUU"* from my mother with her loan balance, but we will buy with the current stock price, so we don't owe her anything, no favors attached.

Maila admitted during our conversation that she hasn't forgiven my mother and father and hasn't let it go.

Repentance – deliverance, and forgiveness have to come!

---

*We had to sell our first home in 2015 because we had a huge conflict between my mother, the reasons were not keeping our mutual agreements and promises; I had to **decide**; our home or hate my mother for the rest of my life. I choose my mother. Maila still was disappointed and didn't forgive as I did.*
These are those moments when we have to make an essential choice; some material things or relationships, doesn't matter what the price is.

We need a real miracle to pay off debts and buy out *"LODJAPUU"* without loans, a real home without any strings.

We also haven't been able to sell *"LODJAPUU"* twice, which means one thing – GOD's *Will* and *Righteousness* must be born! Right now, even if we sell *"LODJAPUU"*, the money belongs to my mother, and the possession is hers. All we have is debt.

2 OCTOBER

What is that we need to understand? Some revelation? Knowing? Faith?

Lord God, help my unbelief, heart of unbelief, and my way of thinking!

I want the Heart of Christ and His way of thinking, the mindset of Christ.

We have six small I loans with companies and three loans with people.

I love the quote: ***"I do make a lot of money, but it doesn't stick to my fingers!"***

> *If I remember correctly, a businessman said it to David Pawson, and it touched me deeply. I really don't know, was that man in Christ or not and how he handles his money and what his motives are, but I still believe that I can own money and **not** love it and not being addicted to it. It's the way we think. Yes, I know that is a very thin path, and **the love of money is the root of all evil [1 Timothy 6:10]**, and for a rich man, it's **hard** to enter the Kingdom of God **[Matthew 19:24]**, but Jesus didn't say **it's not impossible.** It's all about the Will of God and the Heart of man.*
> *I believe that even God needs investors to spread the gospel.*

I love these titles that David Pawson gave when he was invited to speak in seminars for Christian entrepreneurs:
"You can't take it with you; if you could– it would burn."
"How to invest your money beyond the crave."

3 OCTOBER

These are my daily topics, which I wrestle with:
1.) I pray to God without a doubt in the name of Jesus
2.) I accordance with God's Will
3.) "If anyone says to this mountain, 'Go, throw yourself into the sea,' and does not **doubt** in their **heart, but believes** that <u>what they say</u> will happen, it will be done for them. " **[Matthew 17:20&21:21; Mark 11:23]**
4.) A measure of Faith: mustard seed.
5.) That ABBA will be glorified in the Son Jesus **[John 14:13]**
6.) I **decide!**

> Maila went to hairdressers' school, that was her childhood dream, and also, that is a profession that never dies.
> Also, we want to use this to serve Lord God, to serve people and we have to find out how. Our ideas are to serve people in an orphanage, foster homes, nursing home, etc.

ABBA, HELP!!!! What do I have to do?!

4 OCTOBER

My father gave us 20€, so we're able to buy gasoline for a car, but it turns out that Maila's school was canceled because the teacher got ill.
Also, we hoped to receive money from the unemployment fund, but we didn't.

Maila complains to me about the smell of smoke, and for several days now, I felt that I must pray to give this to God and forgive a neighbor – do we have to suffer? Turn the other cheek? **[Matthew 5:39]**
We prayed with Maila about it.

> _As an emotional person_: there has been a battle _inside of me_ to fight for justice and the health of my children. I wanted to take judgment and action in my own hands; so many times, I've wanted to break his jaw so he could never smoke again; I wanted to sue him for harming our health and causing us psychical damage – whatever it comes in our mind to stand for your family. I even thought to curse him. I've made some investments; I bought expensive carbon filters, almost bought HEPA filters, but why I have to spend my money on this? But eventually, I **decided** to **choose** Jesus, no matter how hard it will be.
> **Every action has consequences.**
> And if it's needed, I'm ready to fight. We are not some backboneless Christians.

6 OCTOBER

Two days I haven't woken up at 6 am as I use to every morning, to pray and seek first the Kingdom of God and starting the day with the Lord God. I already feel the emptiness; all the doubts arise about my current situation that I have not been trustworthy **[Luke 16:11]** and that God doesn't give anymore. If you been in the presence of God, and suddenly you're not, then you understand how precious is the devotion to God every day.

Lord God is the **only One** who knows my Heart – He probes my mind and Heart **[Psalm 7:9]** and the only judge!
He knows and is my witness!

7 OCTOBER

I was planning to visit my acquaintance "I" at Otepää (a small town in southern Estonia) where he lives, but I didn't sleep well because my son "N" had a stuffy nose, but I already **decided** on Saturday that I would definitely go! All the train tickets were already bought.

Several times before, I had doubts and hesitations that should I visit him or not, there have been all kinds of obstacles.

> *I met an acquaintance "I" year and a half back in one of the Tallinn's malls, on the children's playground when our boys started to play together, so he started talking to me. I don't believe in coincidences, so I was curious why the Lord God guided him to my path.*
>
> *Also, he was over 50 and needed some help with IT things, and I offered my support.*
>
> *As I know that he's not a religious man, and I consider the possibility that I could "use me", but my only mission was to spread the gospel in the right time and the right place.*
>
> *Everything has a purpose, God uses all people as He pleases, even as a tool to change me.*

8 OCTOBER   TESTIMONY

Way back from Otepää, we visited the Tartu clinic to receive answers to analyze that he made earlier. I was waiting for him in the car while he had to visit the doctor. So, I decided when he gets back; I don't start any conversation. When he got back from the doctor, he had a long face, and it was apparent that he had bad news – an aggressive prostate cancer. He started talking, and all the way back to Tallinn, we spoke of God and the world - he was like a sponge who sucked the gospel from both SALVATION and HELL. He received everything that I spoke of, the Holy Spirit led my mouth so well and expressively, I answered all his questions, and it seemed so logical and understandable to him.

He had ignored all kinds of Christians and Mormons and Jehovah Witnesses since they couldn't answer any of his questions – Praise the Lord, the Holy Spirit gave all the answers he needed at the moment! I felt anointed entirely, talking to a man who had been unbeliever all his life, ignored God, and so on. It was AWESOME!

These are the moment what we have been waiting for – to speak about the gospel in the simplest way with wisdom so that they could receive it. Of course, cancer made his heart softer, and the fear of death made him seek God. What an irony, he got his diagnosis six months after meeting me, and he was a healthy man, according to himself, and he regularly visited the doctor. I knew right away what is causing it and from what he has to repent. I'm not in a hurry, and I want to see what will happen, will he turn his Heart to God or not, will he become humble or not; let him brood a little bit.

*The most important thing is that the gospel can be preached to him. It is up to him to make the **decision**: that's our purpose so that one day standing before the judgment of the Lord God, he cannot say no one has preached the gospel to him or that he is unaware.*

Then we are witnesses, and he doesn't have any excuse!

*"In the same way, **the last will be first**, and the **first will be last**, because **many** are **called**, but **few** are **chosen**."[Matthew 20:16 ISV]*

Yes [ᴸFor], **many** are **invited [called]**, but **only a few** are **chosen."** *[Matthew 22:14].*

*This scripture doesn't say that **"ALL"** are **called**, it says **"many"** and **only a few are chosen**! So, it's not our decision to make, who are the "few"; we just have to spread the gospel [Mark 16:15]*

9 OCTOBER   DECISION

Lord God asked me how serious was I when I said, "**I want you for real**"? You said that after this **decision**, there's no turning back!
I remember you have asked me this question a few times since 2015 when I said, *"I want to receive you **truly and for real!**"*
You have repeated your question so that I could be sure and haven't changed my mind and **decision.**

Let the unbelief become a Faith; let the doubts become wisdom in Faith!
I won't receive any doubts and unbelief!

Honestly? I have no idea what lies ahead, but I know one thing; whatever the price is – **I want Jesus more!**
I **owe Him my life** and my **children's life**; **we belong to Him**.

10 OCTOBER

Eventually, **it all comes down to whether or not the Word of God and the Word of Jesus are true!**
If we don't know the Word, we can't live by it; **Faith without works is dead [James 2:14-26]**

> Just as a ***person's body that does not have a spirit [*** the force of life that animates the body; <u>Gen. 2:7</u>*] is **dead**, so* **faith ·that does nothing [*** without works] **is dead!**

71

11 OCTOBER

As we are in this together with Maila, at stakes is the calling of both of us.

134million € (Superena max lotto Italian lottery)

> *I truly believe that even a lottery jackpot could be a possible way, even if it seems easy money. I see money as a tool to help others, not the purpose*

I will stay in You and You in me!

1.) You make my weakest side the strongest side and a blessing to **many**!
2.) You make me a powerful provider! You fill me with abundance! There is no testimony if there are no sacrifices and no faith!

I have sacrificed all my Heart to You – it belongs to You!

12 OCTOBER

143million € Jackpot – why didn't I win?

In the meantime, it turned out that the SuperMax lottery cannot be played from Estonia, but now it can; hasn't been blocked by EMTA (Estonia Tax and Customs Board) anymore. The question is in gambling taxation; only those who pay gambling tax are allowed to operate in Estonia.

13 OCTOBER

Faith has to grow! More Faith!

How much is *"more faith"*?
What is the measure?
Where does our faith end, and Your faith enters?
Why don't we even have Faith like a mustard seed?
Like Jesus said **[Mark 11:22 DRA]**:

> *And Jesus answering, saith to them: "Have the **faith of God.**"*

14 OCTOBER — VISION of ATTACK; FASTING#1

As I prayed in the morning, in the Spirit: I saw a blood dog who jumped towards me and wanted to attack me behind our 4-meters living room window, and suddenly he disappeared – it was like 2-3 second vision. Utterly demonic, it looked like a colossal Doberman, fangs dripped from the snot (like rabies) and blood. Seeing it made the chills over my back and adrenaline burst over my body.

Today we had a fellowship group meeting. We talked about Christmas. That's the subject that leaves no one cold.

17 OCTOBER — FASTING#4

From today, God gave me the understanding that I have to stop praying for my neighbor - firm **conviction** and **knowledge**.

I don't know what it means, but it has been a long fight and prayer; also, a fight to give it to God, for I have no struggle with "flesh or blood", but... **[Ephesians 6:12]**

> It doesn't mean that I gave up and started to suffer; No – I gave it away from my heart, and I don't seek my own justification, but now I demand Lord God's Righteousness and Justice *[Psalm 11:7; 31:2; 33:5]*. Now I trust His ways and His judgment and His grace and mercy- if needed! Lord God sees more than I do. We have to realize that the Lord God is Almighty, and He is still the same God in Old Testament as in New Testament: He will stand for us and fight the fight for us *[Deuteronomy 3:22;20:4; Romans 8:31]* because we are His **real children**. He is a **Perfect Father** who won't leave us. The **Wrath of Lord God** isn't gone.
> I still want his **soul** to be saved.

---

18 OCTOBER   FASTING#5

I prayed in the morning that God would give Maila winning numbers of Jackpot.

20 OCTOBER   ATTACK; TESTIMONY

Today was speaking about *"Christianity"* on Youth Alpha course at Kohila; in the morning, I had a panic about what I should talk about, and I said: *"dear Lord God, speak for yourself!"*
I started to take notes for myself, some queues, especially when the topic is enormous, and I have only 30 min to talk about Christianity.
So I made slides, for myself and then I had an idea that in the end, I should show them an illustrative and emotional video, so I did; the animation was from Full of Eyes -*"Dead Comes Alive"*.

Before leaving the Youth Alpha course, I had a debate with my mother and father; they asked what way they haven't been supportive?
Father said: *"money is the problem."*;

I replied: *"No-wrong."*
Then he said: *"if there was a lot of money, then there aren't any problems."*
I said: *"Wrong- then there's **mammon**,"* and I left.
On my way to Kohila, I prayed to receive peace.

> *These are "those conversations" when your parents humiliate and accuse that you are doing everything wrong and you so stupid. But they will never understand that I'm not like them, I have my own path to walk and that's my decision to make. But at the same time, they could be supportive and have Faith in me. At the same time, they are discussing if I lost my mind, is there a mental breakdown, etc. They just don't get it, because there is nothing wrong with me.*

Maila today admitted that two nights ago when she saw a video **"23 Minutes in Hell"** from YouTube that I sent her, after praying, she felt that significant burden has been removed and that she has *"released the money"* and payment defaults.
Then came great peace, and she felt how the Holy Spirit filled her with Agape Love for other people that she has never felt before. Now she can love neighbor, and now she can and dare to talk about God, the block was gone (*sometimes I have noticed that she seems ashamed to talk about Jesus*).
Amen, what a testimony!

Maila wrote:

> *"In the evening, Henry sent me to watch a video of Bill Wiese"* **23 Minutes in Hell.** *"*
> *After watching the video, I prayed and felt happy and Agape's Love to love neighbors and not be ashamed to tell others about Christ. I felt like I have let go of money, and I gave all my worries to God! Experienced Peace. "*

Being truly honest - how many times have we **ashamed Jesus?** *The Gospel? I was too many times. Because the enemy repeats all the time that we are some stupid fairy tale's believers, and it's time to grow up; also, Jesus has been imagined in the world as a soft longhaired man who even doesn't hurt a fly. That's the image we have of him, as Jesus being like a woman with long hairs: that's a devil's job to make him like "Babyface", not a* **real** *man! Who wants Lord God like that?!*

No! He is not even close to what we imagine and picture. I believe that in our world, as a man, he looked precisely like **Akiane Kramarik** *saw Him and painted.*

First - *long hair is only for women not for men* **[1 Corinthians 11:14-16]** *and* **long hair are shameful ["disgrace" ESV; "dishonor" ASV] for man,** *but* **glory to woman!**

Second thing - **He has RISEN!** *Also, we can see that after He had risen, He* **changed His appearance** *so that people didn't recognize Him* **[Mark 16:12]** *One day, He will return to* **judge** *with the Wrath of God! And the "baby Jesus" that we worship at Christmas? He has been already grown-up, and He will return! We have to take it seriously that there is a* spiritual world; *and if there is a spiritual world there are also* spiritual bodies **[1Corinthians 15:42-54]**

We can't just imagine them and ignore that they are mighty creatures. *Take as example Angels; the first words from all Angels were* **"Fear not" [Daniel 10; Luke 1:13; Revelation 1:17]**

John's vision of Christ in "the Book of Revelation" is terrifying **[Revelation 1:9-18]**

We must not take it as allegory or any fairy tale! *They are real!*

We have to realize whom we are dealing with.

It is always easier to make images of what we are worshipping; we just "need" these to be under our noses, to see, and whom to turn to. It is deceptive [Exodus 20:4]

We have to be proud that Jesus is our Savior and confess Him before the people and let go of fear and shame what others

> think about us! If we don't, then Jesus won't either! *[Matthew 10:32; Luke 12:8]*

21 OCTOBER   DREAM of STEALING

<u>Maila had a dream about stealing – at first, that dream seemed so unimportant:</u>

> *"Henry and I went to the countryside, where were people's gardens, their greenhouses, and their garden beds lay. It was in the daytime. There were only a couple of ladies working, and on the other side, there were so-called caravans. We walked in the garden, and we took some products, such as tomatoes, onions, without asking for permission. It seemed that there's nothing wrong with it. However, we were noticed that we aren't locals, and we didn't have our own garden bed, so the guard was called, and we had to explain why we're here and what we were doing. Henry wore a blue hoodie with front pockets, full of some products, which he just gave away in the end. We didn't need these so much; it wasn't a matter of life and death. Everything went smoothly, and wc just walked away.*
> *In the end, did we have something in our pockets, or were they empty? Don't know the answer. "*

When Maila told me about the dream, I knew exactly what she was talking about!

The Holy Spirit said that **I am a thief**! The way He said; it wasn't injustice, but in peace and with Agape Love. In fact, he reminded me of what I already forgotten.

I ran up to the second floor right away and started destroying everything related to piracy – I have been a *"legal"* pirate for over ten years. Even from the *"PRO versions"* of the programs, I just tried them, but didn't use them, I downloaded movies that I liked but didn't distribute them - everything seemed so "innocent."

I repented of everything, and I gave away these **"shelters"** and **"fortresses"** from my heart, and I gave away all the movies. All my heart belongs to You, Lord God!

The movies have been **"little idols"** They were those little **"fortresses"** or **"shelter"** that filled my emptiness, the injustice that exists in the world, evoked a sense of justice and the *"the good guys always win"* emotions.

All the movies were deleted, as well as programs and data from my previous jobs.

I lied - I deceived on my previous employer when I left work on the last day. I deliberately deleted all the information from my work laptop, which I had to give away the next day. I fully cleaned the computer, but before that, I made backups for myself so that one day I could use it for learning and analyze the information as a hobby.

The former boss said I have to leave everything in the information, but I already deleted all from the computer, so I told him, but I never told him that I made backups.

Of course, I justified myself that the information belongs to me, and it was my researches.

> *If I ever need it, I will confess to him if I meet him one day. Yes, I struggled with shame, and because of my reputation, but it's not about me, it's about the righteousness of God!*

My father said that just before Maila's dream, they spoke with a mother that I'd been basically stolen, accused me of stealing - we were talking about loans and debts. Stealing is stealing; the loan is the loan. He said that Pawson stamped the borrower who doesn't pay back as stealing. There is a big difference here - **intentional** action is **stealing**, I will pay back all my loans, it will take time, but I will do it with the Lord God! I have borrowed with a sincere heart that I will also pay back every dime! It's all about an **Attitude of Heart**, always!

> *Being in debt is so embarrassing: the worst part is if you owe to a fellow Christian, to a brother in Faith and if he is also your best friend. There's saying: "if you want to get rid of your friend, just borrow him money. "*
>
> *Even if you explain the situation and ask for forgiveness, still there will be a tension in between, because what we do when we lend money? We're waiting to repay.*
>
> *I believe that's all about our mindset: if you lend money, don't wait for it to repay- let it go! Borrow like you never see the money! Don't let the borrowers know that!*
>
> *If you can't lend with a heart like that, then <u>do not do this at all</u>! If they repay it's excellent, if they don't- <u>forgive them </u>and let them go from chains. Paying back is the borrower's concern and the attitude of the heart!"*
>
> *"The **wicked** borrow and do not repay, but the righteous are gracious and giving [Psalm 37:2] "*
>
> *That's the first mistake that we as Christians do! I've seen it so many times. Eventually, these are our "bad experiences" that bring forth disappointments.*
>
> ***Just be a giver, not the lender! [2 Corinthians 9:7]***
> *As owing to a brother or a friend applies the same thing- friendship is worth priceless [Proverbs 18:19]*
> ***I will instead be a slave of Christ than a man [1 Corinthians 7:23]***

---

23 OCTOBER   DELIVERANCE

I had a conversation with my mother, and she admitted that she didn't want to sell *"LODJAPUU"* at all, so perhaps a simple answer to why *"LODJAPUU"* couldn't be sold - she didn't want to because she has the Authority and it belongs to her!

I said: *"God has no problem bringing us this right buyer."*
My mother asked: *"Why didn't you sell then?"*

I replied: *"Because **you** didn't **want** to!"*

Unfortunately, she didn't say anything about it until now; it was like an ice-cold shower to me, and suddenly everything was clear why nothing worked, and I just pushed and pushed and never went through. I can't do anything against her will. Previously we had the understanding that she trusted me and gave permission to sell it.
I really believed that the selling *"LODJAPUU"* would be easy because I have a favoring from the Lord God, and miracles are possible.
I have told my mother many times that we have to sell *"LODJAPUU"* so that she could get rid of the loans, and right now is the best time to do it because there are hard times ahead. We must take advantage of the market price, and for the rest of the money, we can build a separate little house next to the mother's home. She has over a hectare of land.
The priority was to set my mother free from loans!
But now I didn't achieve my goal and taking loan to finish things was mistake.

I god thinking…Why are we so afraid to call things by the right names; I mean, why do we lie to ourselves? ***"By continually lying, we end up believing a lie ourselves."***
In the end, we ignore the truth, and we no longer make differences between truth and lie.

---

24 OCTOBER   **SHORT REVIEW**

Short review:

1.) Repentance 6 August from DEBT and MONEY – The mindset.
2.) Repentance 21 October of theft, fortifications, and places of refuge

An interesting phenomenon - if I repent, there will be comfortable and liberating! And it stays!

ABBA, I WANT TO BE RIGHT TO YOU!

25 OCTOBER

Arguing with my father again: he talks about "accusations."
I don't blame anyone! Never!
Everything I have done, debt, pride, etc. – Is my entire fault!
Only I made these decisions! Only I am responsible for all this!

> *But it's an interesting phenomenon- consciously and rationally, you know that it's wrong and it's understandable. But still, you're deceived and like a black bag gets pulled over your head, and you lose consciousness, control, and then you discover that you're in a different place, like a memory cap, hearing the lie that "everything will be fine" and "you can pay", etc. That's not the **voice of God**; this voice doesn't want you to panic when the ship is sinking, but to calm you down and fool you so that you may not resist. Even at the bottom of the ocean, the same voice repeats that everything is ok, so you won't start to swim.*

Through the **BLOOD OF JESUS**, we are pure and RIGHT before Jehovah!

27 OCTOBER

I went to church, so many confirmations, and the Holy Spirit asked, *"Do we only believe with our minds, or do we believe with our hearts, with every cell?"*

We **know**, but we don't **believe**!

I choose to believe with my heart - I am fervent! Fervent for Holy Spirit.

30 OCTOBER

Doubt - repeated asking is doubt – sometimes it is like a mantra; the words that we continuously repeat- but the heart does not believe and are full of doubts. We even get used to it. Yes, it has to reach **from our mouth to the heart**!

> *And sometime we have to repeat and pray for breakthrough, so that it may reach from our mouth to the heart. We need this "click" in our heart, that "I know that I know that I know…"*

FAITH - I DECIDE TO BELIEVE!

Maila's sister visited us, and we talked about God.

31 OCTOBER

The Superena Max Jackpot is (tomorrow) 300 mln € on Saturday. I'm crazy, and I believe it belongs to me now! That would be a powerful testimony, Faith without actions is dead **[James 2:14-20]**

I talked to Maila so that there should be no doubts.

2 NOVEMBER

We didn't win the Superena Jackpot; I woke up at 3:00 a.m. to pray and let God organize it, trusting Him.
I decided to BELIEVE!

On the way home from a birthday party, I saw an ex-girlfriend "**K**", driving by; it seemed to be some kind of sign, an anomaly like *Déjà vu*. Like a *"black cat running over the street"* kind disbelief. Some weird feeling struck through me; I haven't seen her for about ten years. I'm glad that she's all right, but I still believe that these things have been unfinished or, well, trying to be forgotten. A strange experience, it doesn't matter which of my previous girlfriends—a story without an end.

We think that when we break up from previous relationships, that's it. No, they are endless stories, and often they are unfinished. However, I am referring to precisely those "breaking-up's" where hearts are broken; otherwise, there was no love.

There will be a mark forever, a scar in the heart.

One of my ex-girlfriend "L" said: *"I forgive, but I will not forget"*; my compassion for her.

---

*I had two most important relationships in the past; I mean two girls; one was "**L**" and another one was "**K**."*

That 2005-2007 was the hardest time that I had.

*I had a relationship with "**L**" before "**K**," and it lasted about three years, and "**L**" became <u>pregnant</u>, and I was so happy, I wanted to become a father at a young age like my parents.*

*But "**L**" was in the middle of finishing high school, and she was so depressed because of the upcoming exams, <u>and **she had to decide whether to finish school with a "silver medal" or become a mother**</u>. Unfortunately, <u>she decided to have an **abortion.**</u> I don't blame anybody. If I could, it would be myself.*

I still remember how we went to the doctor, and I sat behind the doctor's door.

*I knew that <u>something inside of me died</u> on that day. **It is indescribable, the emptiness inside of me that changed my life and shattered love.** I believe that she experienced the same thing. When you realize it, then it's too late.*

<u>Regret</u> will follow your broken heart.

Our relationship also died on that day.

After some time, "**K**" found me from the internet and we met, we hadn't seen each other for about five years.

When I first met **"K"**, when I was about 16 years old in the camp. It turned out that she lived a few blocks away from me, and we started dating for about a few weeks, and then she vanished.

So, when she found me, and we met, I fell in love with a blink of an eye.

I saw a new life, a new opportunity, and new love.

On the same day, I met "**L**," and I left her. I still remember the shock on her face, and she begged me not to leave her, and I felt guilty to leave her. I couldn't resist the guilt, and it ate my conscience for over a year.

That's how started our triple nightmare that lasted about 1,5 years.

I **lied** day after day, minute after minute. At first, it ate my conscience, but in time, the pain increased, and it started to affect my temper. I began drinking every week.

It wasn't just that I lied. I <u>had sex with them at the same time</u>, with "**L**" in the morning or noon, with "**K**" in the evening. I tried to keep it in secret over a year. That feeling, when you know that may get caught, <u>started to create adrenaline.</u>

To avoid suspicion, I figured out different and convincing excuses.

-Yes-, you may say that **<u>I was an adrenaline sex addict whore</u>, <u>fornicator</u>, and it was true.**

I even tried to escape to the army for a year, but that didn't work, Lord God never left me and had another plan; basically, they throw me out.

At the same time, I went to the congregation, and I never took them or any girl that I loved, with me. The faith was too personal for me: maybe I was embarrassed because of the way I acted, and I considered myself Christian.

*Eventually, they both realized I was a **cheater**. I lost both. The damage that I made was indescribable. I wanted "**K**" back and to make things right because I loved her. But the damage was irreversible. About a year later, I met her, and I asked for forgiveness. She forgave me, at least she told it. Only new love could make things new. So she has. That was my first repentance.*

*After that, years later, I wanted to understand what went wrong and **why**; I started to analyze myself so that I could be a better man in the future. It took a year to understand where it came from.*

*And I did find the **answers**.*

*<u>But the weird thing is:</u> All this time, **Lord God never left me and never judged!** He **warned** me that if I continued, someone would die. Not that the Lord God wanted; it's because of my **<u>action has consequences.</u>** And almost did.*

He is Amazing; He is Merciful. I should be dead and burn in hell, but He changed me. He gave me life and gave back the purpose. God doesn't just "do a thing", He has a plan. He is perfect.

Why can't I get "it"?

I still got feeling that the question about *"stealing"* is not over; I asked my friend "**F**" that does he still have my stuff on his external hard drive that I used five years ago? He said:*" Yes"*, and I let him delete them.

<u>It's incredible</u>: Right away when I made Repentance about stealing, God himself began to show where my *"treasures"*,

"fortresses", "refuge" are hidden:
My mother called and complained that her computer's hard drive is full, and I wondered how it could be. When I was checking the computer, I discovered hidden movies, even Christian films, my favorite ones: *"Noah", "Fireproof"," I can only imagine", "GOD is Not Dead 1&2",* etc.
Also, one day my grandfather complained that his tablet went crazy, and some essential apps didn't work, just in case I checked space in the tablet; again, some movies were there. Amazing! Not only that, I still had my own folder on my father's computer, which had been there for years. I had over seven hard drives! Everything has been deleted!

Conclusion: *if you* **decide** *to repent, it has to be* **perfect** *– He will help; in my case, He led me to places I had already forgotten or deliberately well-hidden until everything is deleted. This is an example of these* **"Fruits"** *of Repentance.*

I saw a **vision** in the Spirit, a picture - **when I got the money, Maila divorced me and left with half of the money** - the question was - *"how do I feel, was getting the money the right thing to do or should I make another choice?*
Family or money? I knew with peace of mind that Maila must decide for herself if she wants to go or not.
Money is an AMPLIFIER.

4 NOVEMBER

I told Maila about yesterday's picture and question. The first reaction was that she said that it is not from God, I replied that it doesn't matter – it is still the right question and will remain as a question!
Maila asked me the same question: *"which one would I choose: family or money?"* I replied that, "there is "*something*" inside of people that **can be amplified with money** because otherwise,

everything inside of you would be fine.

That "*something*" must come out now, not when the end times of the "Book of Revelations" are here, and I need her the most! We have to prepare ourselves and being on the same page.

> *That "something" could be ambition, lust, love of money, the passion of the flesh, etc.*
> *If I have to choose: my wife, who goes to hell or path to Heaven: I choose Heaven!*

But I believe that God has put us together for a reason, as we are still together, and when we've been through this, then the wealth isn't an issue.

I said to Maila: "First, the enemy tries to divide ourselves in poverty, creating poverty; if he can't, then wealth!"

I told Maila that from tomorrow I would make 4-day fasting and Euro jackpot is 79 million euros on Friday. Maila said she wants to join me, which was a big surprise! UNITY! **UNITY!**

When family, wife, and husband **agree on something**, **in one mindset,** even more-**prayer** and **fasting** together – then there is **nothing impossible**!

> *That's interesting – many couples divorce after years of marriage; they have forgotten all the battles that they have won and gone through, raising children with their problems, etc. It should be the opposite: all of these experiences should unite them, not divide them!*
> *Of course, every battle unites people and should understand the value of **the Unity**. In such situations, experiences, feelings do not matter – emotions mislead! Most important is that you have somebody that you can trust and go through and being grateful.*

Parents send all kinds of job offers - I believe that in this situation, where we are SO CLOSE, it is the enemy's will that I go to work and end of the story. An enemy doesn't want us to receive what God has **PROMISED** –in <u>my case</u>; I don't receive it if I go to work.

We are praying and fasting together!

If God wanted me to go to work now, it would all have an end - The question immediately arises, why didn't you let me get a job before? I tried for four months, everywhere, even through acquaintance and friends - all the doors were closed!

NB! One thing must be understood immediately - *working* **is not bad** – *working* **is necessary!** In fact, it was one of the first curses that had been put on **man** by throwing Eden out of the garden **[Genesis 3:17-19].**

But a person needs a job, an activity – necessary for growth– have a *goal*! Without a purpose human just fades away, and life loses meaning.

On order:

1.) I am a *son of God* [Romans 8:14]
2.) Authority
3.) Faith
4.) Words
5.) No doubts

We finished our fasting.

I have realized that **I have never honored my father [Exodus 20:12],** we have talked about it for years, and I've denied it because I don't have anything against my father consciously.
But, when I was a young child, my mother agitated me against my father – because parents became parents too young so that they didn't know how to be parents.
Father and mother always fought (my father considered it a spiritual struggle for years) because my father was Christian, and my mother wasn't. Spiritual clash and then my mother used me against my father as a weapon to achieve her goals, her will; I told him to get lost, etc. - My father thought that when I'm already a 12-13-year-old boy, it's *"right time"* to start teaching me and start playing the role of "father" - it's too late! I had a question: "where were you sooner?"
The same pattern I notice on my children: my son doesn't honor Maila and me, and then the Spirit said: *"**You cannot demand your son to honor you if you do not honor your own parents!"***

*I may call it even "**worldwide pandemic**" – The problem of **dishonoring our parents** is rapidly growing. But it is our own fault as parents: we spoiled our children, not discipline them from the beginning, we have our fears and societal pressures that we cannot discipline our children. That is the work of the devil. So that our children will dishonor us and will hate us and rebel. Then finally, they grow apart from us. Even Lord God **disciplines/chastened/punishes** his children, and there is no democracy! [Hebrews 12:5-17].*
Worst case scenario – our child may lose life [Ephesians 6:1-3]:

> „Children, **obey your parents as the Lord wants** [*L* in the Lord], because this is the right thing to do [right; just]. **² The command** says, **"Honor your father and mother [Ex. 20:12; Deut. 5:16]." This is the first command** that has a promise with it— **³** "Then everything will be well with you, and **you will have a long life** on the earth [Ex. 20:12; Deut. 5:16]."

It's one of God's <u>Commandment</u>!
It's not something you can play with and touch the limits of the borders, and play with **God's patience** and **grace.**
Disobedience and **dishonoring** will bring **curse** upon.

8 NOVEMBER

79million € (Did you say not to buy this week but rather buy next week when its 90million €?)

Tomorrow is my younger's son "N"s birthday and I prayed for that no unholy or satanic enemy could come and had no right to come or rule. Honestly, do not want a neighbor to come. Since our youngest child is almost as old as the neighbor's daughter "K", they hang out friendly, and they have always invited us to a birthday out of solidarity. But the question is, what spirituality people carry with them? Who is in leading them?

> By the way, our neighbor's daughter's name "K" is the same as my ex-girlfriend "K"s? What an irony, I believe that there are no coincidences, but time will tell.

9 NOVEMBER

As I previously prayed about "N"s birthday, neighbor girl "K" came only with her father, which was a total surprise.
(*I've always wondered which of neighbor's spirituality is worse, whether the man's or the woman's; one is always more dominant than another. Also, they consider themselves Christians (so said my mother, but I don't like rumors),* but she doesn't want to get married, and she loves horror movies, etc.
She makes a very modest impression, but it deceives people!
So, she couldn't come, and he smiled and raised his shoulders, said as an excuse that *"she needs her quality time."* I was pretty sure it would be the other way around.
That is only confirmation that the *"enemy"* couldn't come!
During our conversation about marriage, he admitted that they are Christians, but she doesn't want to get married *(I'm talking about the same neighbor whom we have smoking problems).*

> *I'm not talking about people; I still talk about the* **spirituality** *that* **they wear***. It means under what* **Spirit's Authority** *and* **influence** *they act and live* **[Ephesians 6:12];** *whom they serve because everybody serves somebody!*

10 NOVEMBER   MAILA's DREAM

Maila had a dream:

> *"Anre came to visit us and that he has a gift to see the spiritual world and see open "portals" as known as "doors/gateways". And one of these portals was in our backyard; the portal was between two tall trees, and it was about 3 meters high. So, Anre asked me:" Henry, I see the* **portal** *on your backyard, and do you* **agree** *with such a situation?"*

> *But I replied: "It doesn't bother me since it's outside not inside of our house, and our house is protected."*
> *Anre said: "If you don't care, you will **burn**!"*

11 NOVEMBER

I have the Authority to close the portals! Now I know where the blood dog came from, whom even my youngest son "N" saw: One day my son "N" pointed a finger outside the window and said *"auhhti"* (it means a *"dog"*; he's only 2) and ran into my arms like he was scared. Then I asked: *"where?"* And I realized that he saw the same diminished blood dog and I right away rebuked it, and it was gone. I asked my son does he still sees it or not, and he said: *"No"* (we have 4 meters wide panorama window).

I called Anre, and I talked to him about the blood dog I saw in the Spirit on 14 October, who was behind the window, I thought I'd ask because "N" said that *"auhhti"* were behind the window and ran to me to hide.

I caught a moment and took "N" to my arms, and we went to the window and asked if he saw *"auhtii"* and said *"yes"*, then I prayed, I rebuked and then disappeared – "N" said that it was gone.

I suddenly remembered Maila's dream about the *"portals"*; by the way, Maila saying that she knew nothing of the *"portals"* or any such word before that!

Anre said that he also saw a dog and asked what it looked like, I said it was similar to a Dobermann, then he googled and told that this is precisely what he saw himself a long time ago. He promised to take the matter seriously and pray and give me an answer, what it might mean.

> *We often deal with the **consequences**, which are repeated; the house is constantly on fire, we extinguish it, but we ignore the cause, do not want or do not dare to investigate the reason, by*

> asking: *"**WHY?**"*
> *The "door/portal of the spiritual world" is open all the time, and from the open door comes all things which we have to deal with. We rebuke and fight against the enemy, but never close the door: they come and go how they please, we throw them out, but worse will come back **[Luke 11:24-26]**. We lack fighting skills: yes, Paul gave us passages about Armor of God **[Ephesians 6:13-18]**, and Jesus gave Authority **[Luke 10:19]** in His name **[Mark 16:17]**, but we need to **know how and when to use them!** You need the wisdom of the Holy Spirit. One little thing, the Armor of God, isn't for attacking, searching the enemy; it's for **defense and counter-attack! It's for winning battles, and war is for the Lord God!** Lord God will end it **[Revelation 20:9-10]**, and it's not our job to do! And there is a reason for that. But the devil is already beaten.*

12 NOVEMBER

I feel this door is a small thing; Jehovah is BIG!
Jesus taught us to pray to the Father ABBA! NOT to the Holy Spirit or Jesus!
Blood of the Sacrifice of Jesus! Blood Cover of Jesus!

13 NOVEMBER

ABBA FATHER!!!

To ask for something from the Father in Jesus' name, we must also have a mandate! Pawson said that we must pray **as Jesus** did! It has a point, but Jesus said we would ask in **His name,** and the Father will do - It does not work for fools, of course. Understandably, it is also possible to get an *"NO"* answer from the ABBA Father, and that's also the answer!

> *There's only one **exception**, when we could get the answer "NO" **[James 4:3]**:*
>
> > *„Or **when you ask, you do not receive** because ·**the reason you ask is wrong** [or you ask with the wrong motives; ᴸ you ask badly/wrongly]. You want things so you ·can **use** [ᴸ spend] them for **your own pleasures**."*

How to receive and pray in Jesus' name, as Jesus said?

There are several preconditions for this:
1.) FAITH –Mustard seed **[Luke 17:5-6]**
2.) STATUS- Who are you? **[Romans 8:15; John 1:12]**
3.) MANDATE (like Pawson said) – In the Name of Jesus

I **repent** and ask ABBA for forgiveness that I did not listen to or trust when He said when I left my previous job, that I would not deceive using a "fixed-term contract" to withdraw unemployment benefits from the Unemployment Insurance Fund;
So that I would trust ABBA to come out with a resignation! I would be fair, but I knew it's - I knew it was nonsense and wrong, and I didn't do that! I was a **coward** because I am responsible for two children and my wife.
I didn't trust ABBA!

I accept from ABBA the Father all the punishment I deserve because I love Jehovah's **Truth** and **Justice** more than my own life. Amen!

> **STATUS** - *Who are you then? Many Christians say that they are **God's tools**, but I have a question for you: <u>Are you **God's tool** or **God's child**</u>?*

I started to look for an answer to the question: *"How do I receive the Authority and the Faith to move mountains and have no doubt?"*

1.) Jesus confesses *and* acknowledges me before ABBA the Father **[Matthew 10:32-33; Luke 12:8-9]**
Question is: Does Jesus confesses *and* acknowledges us before the ABBA the Father?
NB! What if one day as a **Christian, Jesus** tells us that **He doesn't know us**, even if we have done so many miracles in His name **[Matthew 7:22-23; Matthew 25:12-13; Luke 13:23-27]**
Jesus is talking about Christians!
I pray that this Revelation will open all the Christian's eyes of the Heart! It's a matter of life and **death, 2nd death! [Revelation 21:8]**

Jesus **longs** that you would get to know **Him personally**, that would be your **yearning** to understand **Him** and the **Father**. Not because of the *fear or pressure* or *fear of hell* or not that *"I must"* come to salvation -No! But *your motive* comes from the deepest desire of your heart.

2.) Faith – **Faith** is an **act**! Faith without works is dead **[James 2:14-26]**
3.) Doubt is War! **War in mindset.**

I remembered the story of Jacob with Esau, when Jacob wrestled with God and didn't' let go and didn't surrender, even if you know that you can't win! **[Genesis 32:22-32]**

I feel like I'm in the same situation, maybe I am crazy to seek **first** the Kingdom of Heaven above all **[Matthew 6:33]**

Are we **really God's children**? Does the Spirit testify that we are God's Children**?**
I've been thinking about that scripture so many times to analyze my own heart.
Driving my son to kindergarten, I heard a pastor talking about the same thing on the radio. **There are no coincidences!**

The question is: *are we still God's children*? The enemy is fighting to keep us from being God's children.

Why is this question so crucial? It's not just confessing that we are God's children or not; ***it's about living it****: there are* **conditions***, and we ignore these, or we make them generalize them.*
The conditions are*: Doing the* **will of Heavenly Father.** *Jesus confessed so many times that he is doing the Will of God, not his own.* ***[John 6:38]*** *Also, Jesus said, that's who's doing the* **will of God** *is brother, sister, mother* ***[Mark 3:35]***
The same applies to **"Love***,*** *and we are talking about* **"Agape":**
God's love *is conditional!*
The conditions are:
The same as previous: doing the will of God and keeping commandments and keeps Jesus' words, and also: we have to love Him! [John 14:21,23,27] These are Jesus' words!
We are often over flooded by the slogan "God's loves is unconditional", supported by the scripture of John 3:16:"

"[- For] God **loved** *the world so much that he gave his one and only [only; unique;* T*only begotten; 1:14, 18] Son so that whoever* **believes** *in him may not be lost [*T*perish], but have eternal life."*

If we even analyze it:
First: *it says,* ***"loved"*** *in the* **past tense***; Yes, He loved it when He created the world, and everything was perfect- man and woman also! And He still loves humans as a creation. He didn't say that "**loves**" as the present time.*
Secondary*: He loved "**the world,**" and there is not specifically said that "humans nor people" or "man" or "woman".*
Third: *"**believes in Him**" is a condition! You have to believe in Him,* **so** **it's for Christians!**
Jesus himself says **[John 17:9 EHV]***:*

> *"I pray for* **them***. I am not praying for the* **world***, but for* **those** *you have given me, because* **they are yours.**

*And we put so much emphasis on that "**God is Love**", but we forget that He is also with* **Holy Anger [Romans 1:18-19],** *and He is the ONE who Judges!*
Of course, God is Love **[1 John 4:7-8]***, the source of Love, and He created it; it doesn't self-produce. The world was made by Love.*
We *and our* **free will** *are a testimony of His Love!*
But we even forget that Lord God may **hate** *somebody* **[Romans 9:15; Malachi 1:2-3]** *not only something* **[Proverbs 6:16-19]**
Let us never become part of the **Wrath of God.**

19 NOVEMBER   DREAM

I had a dream that I went to a job interview at a school opposite the Methodist Church and Tallinn University. It turned out to be the most significant international Christian school. It would be cool to match the *"home learning platform"* with this.
The school was like a center point of all Christian schools:

influential Christian school, I saw many young people sizzling back and forth in the lobby, and the right hand had a buffet labeled *"Jesus feeds."*
It has been my dream to build a Christian school for years.

This week Eurojackpot is 90 million €, and Superena Max is over 300 million €.
Jeshuah Hamoshia, through the sacrificial blood, it's ours!
Authority.

20 NOVEMBER   REPENTANCE

I listened to a sermon about *"Your Staff (stick)"* by the Belarus pastor as I drove to Otepää by train. The preaching was a testimony and reminder of God's grace and miracles, also about remembering God's works and about copying others.
We forget so quickly what God has done for us, all the fights and winnings and grace and the miracles. Why do we forget to be grateful?
Many Christians copy each other, such as charismatic and well-known preachers, as well as their experiences. *"If they succeeded in something, so will I."* This is hazardous thinking and making such conclusions; we do it subconsciously.

In the evening, Anre called, and we spoke about the blood dog, and he mentioned that maybe I have "something" against our Pastor. I said that I would call him back tomorrow.
My stomach began to twist that "something" started to raise its head.

Maila's sister called, and we spoke about Christmas.

The Holy Spirit revealed that I've been mistaken against my Pastor, deceived him, lied, etc. I was revealing my Pastor's and internal affairs of the congregation to another pastor!

I left my home church to find another with my wife because there were things in our church that I didn't like, and I was against.

It doesn't matter what those things were, ordinary things, disappointments in one thing or another. I met my pastor before leaving and said everything from the bottom of my heart that I disagreed with, and I felt I needed to go. I remember it so clearly when he asked if I was leaving because of these things, and I said: "No." In fact, it was still a disappointment. And yet I knew I couldn't be part of what I'm against of! My pastor has a good heart, and he was very understanding, and he said that I could come back whenever I'm ready. He also said that sometimes we have to leave to find the answers and find the "right home church".

As my pastor said something like that: "<u>All churches are perfect until you step in.</u>"

*And I agree, our **motives** matter, **our heart**! Why we do something that we do?*

In all churches and congregations, have something that we don't like, but what we can to make differences? Or is it even possible?

The problem is that we grow in the Spirit, our eyes will be opened more and more, and the Holy Spirit shows wrong things, not because to judge or rebel, but to change it. That's the hard truth, but yes, we can't be runaways all the time and searching the "right church/congregation" all our lives.

Yes, I agree that there are also extreme situations and you really have to leave, and you find a new home immediately where you experience the presents of the Holy Spirit, and yes-there are churches and congregations from which the Holy Spirit has long gone, and it's just a plastic bag full of air and man-powered.

We are… at least; we meant to be the Body of Christ; it doesn't matter which part, but we have to be part of! And it's crucial to hear the Voice of Holy Spirit, so that He may guide us and tell us what we have to do; don't be afraid, if He shows things that are wrong and only you are who can change it! And if He shows, believe me, He will provide you with all His **Power** and **Wisdom** and **Gifts**!

12 Christ gave those **gifts** to prepare [*L* ...to equip] God's holy people for the work of serving, to **make the body of Christ stronger**. **13** This **work** must continue until we are **all joined together in the same faith** [**or all reach unity in the faith**] and in the **same knowledge** of the Son of God. We must become like a mature person [*or the perfect Man; C Christ*], **growing until we become like Christ** and have **his perfection** [*L to the measure of the stature of Christ's fullness*].
14 Then <u>we will no longer be babies</u> [*children*]. <u>We will not be tossed about like a ship that the waves carry one way and then another</u>. **We will not be ·influenced by every new teaching** [*L carried along by every wind of (false) teaching*] we hear from people who are trying to ·fool [*trick*] us. They make plans [*scheme*] and try any kind of trick to fool people into following the wrong path [*error; false teaching*]. **[Ephesians 4:12-14]**

Also, we have to understand that when we **grow**, we **eat** and one day we feel that that the **milk** isn't for us anymore **[1 Corinthians 3:2; Hebrews 5:11-14]** and we need **solid food**, but we don't get it without learning and studying the **Word of God by ourselves**!
I thought years that it's enough for me to live on preachers and pastors speeches and sermons by not reading myself what the Word says. When I read, it seemed so **dry**, and I didn't understand the true meaning, and it made me **lukewarm**. It was much better to hear and eat with my ears the speeches that pastors or preachers talked about, it was useful to my ears, and I **listened** to what **I wanted**. Especially I liked the Evangelists from another country (basically from the US), and I was eager to hear what the Lord God wants to tell me through

evangelist. Time after time, I would get tired of American evangelists, who wanted at the end of the sermons "lot of five hundred" (it was years ago), tired of the same message. It all just started a quick thirst for the Lord God, but it even quickly disappeared. It is the same as with children if you give them lots of sugar, and the sugar punch lasts just a short time, and that's it.

Then you ask yourself: **"is it all?"**

(I still wait that day when the Lord God will lift up somebody from our own country (Estonia), it doesn't have to be one person, but it all starts from one)

That is why we **must grow in the Word of God**; not in other words, it doesn't matter who he is. That is one reason why we disappoint in pastors is that we don't know the Word, and we don't know Jesus **personally**. _We rely on pastors and preachers, not on the Word of God!_ And if something happens with the pastor, for example, we discover that he is "false teacher" and you see that you have been deceived **[2 Peter 2:1]**, we run away in frustration and despair, we are also disappointed in God, and we leave our churches because of the pastors? Do we choose the pastor over Jesus? Or we choose disappointment and forsake Jesus and our Faith? What is **worth our faith** then? **[1 Timothy 4:1-2]**

Of course, there are "churches and congregations" that want to keep control and influence over us, so that you cannot leave, if you want, they will make a fool of you or something worse. They see you as "money" and money keeps their pockets full. Sometimes we even have to reveal them **[Ephesians 5:11]**, but _according to God's Will and Wisdom._

Maybe they started the church or congregation in the Spirit, but they finished without Him. There may be a couple of reasons; one is **money** and **fame**. Another is a **sin**.

It doesn't matter how you start; matters how you will finish!
BUT they _forget one crucial thing_: **The Judgment _starts from_**

the House of God (churches and congregations)! [1 Peter 4:17]

*"There used to be false prophets <u>among God's people</u> [<u>Deut. 13:1–5</u>; <u>18:14–22</u>; <u>Jer. 28</u>] just as you will have some **false teachers ·in your group** [^L among you; <u>Jude 4</u>]. They will **secretly teach** [bring in; introduce] things that are **wrong—teachings** that <u>will cause people to be lost</u> [^L <u>destructive heresies/opinions/factions</u>]. They will even refuse to accept [^L deny] the Master [^C Jesus] who bought their freedom [^L them; ^C as a master purchases a slave; <u>1 Cor. 6:20</u>; <u>1 Pet. 1:18</u>]. So they will bring quick ruin [destruction] on themselves. ² **Many will follow their evil** [depraved; debauched; licentious] ways and say evil things about [malign; slander] the way of truth. ³ Those <u>**false teachers only want your money,**</u> so [^L **In their greed**] **they will use [exploit] you by telling you lies [with deceptive/false words].** Their judgment spoken against them long ago is still coming [not idle], and their ruin is certain [does not sleep]. [2 Peter 2:1-3]*

*I know that after ·I leave [my departure; I am gone], ·some people will come like wild wolves [^L wild/savage wolves will come in among you] and ·**try to destroy** [will not spare] the flock. ³⁰ ·Also, [or Even] **some from your <u>own group</u> will rise up and ·<u>twist the truth</u>** [^L speak perversions/distortions] **and will ·lead away [lure; entice] ·<u>followers [disciples]</u> after them**. [Acts 20:29-30]*

My dear children [2:1], ·these are the last days [^L it is the last hour; ^C suggesting urgency, though not claiming the end was *near]. [ᴸ Just as] You have heard that the ·**enemy of Christ** [ᴸ antichrist] **is coming**, and **now many ·enemies of Christ** [ᴸ antichrists; ᶜ false teachers; 2:22; 2 John 7] are already here. This is how we know that ·these are the last days [ᴸ it is the last hour].* **¹⁹ ·These enemies of Christ were in our fellowship, but they left us** *[ᴸ They went out from us;* ᶜ *probably to form a rival fellowship].* **They never really belonged to us** *[ᴸ But they were not of us];* *[ᴸ For]* **if they had been a part of us, they would have ·stayed** *[remained; abided]* **with us.** *But they left, ·and* **this shows** *[or so that it would be shown]* **that none of them really belonged to us.** *[1 John 2:18-19]*

Because **some are from among us,** we have to be **very careful,** and **we must not be deceived because they know the Word of God!** **Everybody could read the bible** – *there's nothing new about it. The* **Pharisees** *and* **Sadducees** *knew Word of God. Even* **devil** *knew Word of God in the desert about 2000 years ago!* **Devil knows the Word of God even better than we. Only thing that separates from them is the Holy Spirit.**

„*who has made us sufficient to be ministers of a* **new covenant, not of the letter but of the Spirit.** *For* **the letter kills,** *but the* **Spirit gives life.**" *[2 Corinthians 3:6 ESV]*

You ·are very patient with *[willingly put up with; gladly tolerate]* **anyone who comes to you and preaches a different Jesus** *from the one we preached.* **You are very willing to accept a spirit that is different from the Spirit you received,** *or* **a gospel that is different** *from the one you ·accepted [or received from us].* *[2 Corinthians 11:4]*

Unfortunately, the damage that they will do is enormous and irreversible.
That's why we need "personal Jesus." *It means Jesus, whom we know **personally**, and the Bible **warns** about that several times - not **personal jesus**, who we make by ourselves, They have become so **arrogant** that they do it in public, not in secret anymore, and people have been deceived because people don't know the Word! It's so easy to fool people!*

*(I believe that the "Awakening" times as we remember, are history. Now will begin "**personal awakening**" times, **personal filling with the Holy Spirit**, and soon will end gatherings like we are used to, but little fellowship groups will rise and expand worldwide, because **persecution** will spread. We have to prepare ourselves! Covid-19 showed pretty well what will happen, if churches and congregations will be permitted and closed.)*

Let's break the ice now:
Women cannot and must not be pastors!
There is so much controversy about it among Christians, but I make it brief:
I don't want to speak about "women submitting to man" scriptures, but I want to refer to Lord God's words and the deception among us, but first:
Few facts:
*1.) Jesus was a **man**, not a woman:*
*2.) Jesus 12 apostles were **men**, not even single of them was a woman.*
And there was a purpose of that:
*3.) Paul **permitted** a woman to teach a **man [1 Timothy 2:11-14]:***

> "Let a woman learn by listening quietly [in silence] and being ready to cooperate in everything [ᴸ in full/all submission]. **¹²** But <u>I do not allow a woman to teach</u> or to have [assume; exercise] **authority** over a man [or her husband], but to listen quietly [be quiet],"

Then **we stop quoting and start to philosophize and interpret however we want or need** at the moment, and don't want to read on:

> **¹³** <u>because Adam wa</u>s formed **<u>first </u>**and then Eve [<u>Gen. 2:8</u>, <u>18</u>, <u>22</u>]. **¹⁴** And **Adam was not tricked** [deceived; led astray], but the **woman was ·tricked** [deceived; led astray] and **became a sinner** [transgressor; <u>Gen. 3:1–6</u>].

That is why "**Christian feminists**" don't want to talk about nor admit.
Now we are talking about **the real reasons because even Christians are accusing Adam of the Fall.**
Paul referred and explained very simply why women could not teach men because **she** is the real reason why the world fell and **<u>she became a sinner!</u>** And then Adam and Eve were cast out of Eden. The **woman was deceived**, not the **man**! And she is not trustful, because she wanted to have authority and control over man:
God himself said to the woman: [Genesis 3:16]

> Then he said to the woman, "I will sharpen the pain of your pregnancy, and in pain you will give birth. And you **<u>will</u>* desire to control** your husband, but he will **rule** over you."

What does it mean? It means that woman **<u>is</u>** (*referring "**will**" in future tense) **jealous** of the man because he was the **first** one, formed by Image of God, and he was pure. We don't know how

long Adam was in the Garden of Eden without a woman
[Genesis 2: 7-20]:

> But Adam [or the man; 1:27] **did not find a helper** that was
> **right for him** [2:18].

> [8] [*For] Man did not come from woman, but woman came
> **from man.** [9] And **man was not made for woman,** but
> **woman was made for man** [Gen. 2:18]. **[1 Corinthians
> 11:8-9]**

But the woman knew that she was made as a **helper** and that
she was **made from** man and **for** man.
So did the serpent as Satan! That is why the serpent
approached to woman, not to a man, because he knew very
well that Adam could not be deceived! And he used a woman as
a "**weakest link**" to deceive and to make people rebel against
the Lord God. (I believe that Adam would have made sushi from
the serpent)
Adam did not blame God, neither justified himself!
[Genesis 3:12]:

> The man said, "You gave this woman to me and she gave me
> fruit from the tree, so I ate it.

Rather he **explained**, "why should I have not trusted woman
whom you gave me?" It was a sincere heart and rather "cry out":
"why not, you gave me her, so I trusted her!"

Why do we think and say that Adam blamed God for giving a
"deceitful" woman?
He didn't! Why? Reason is very simple:
1.) We think with our sinful mind and living in the sin, it's our
nature to blame. We blame Adam, because we didn't know him

and his relationship with God.

2.) Adam was perfect man – He wasn't **born**, he was **made!**
He was **without sin**, because there was no sin and he was
made from **image of Elohim.**

3.) He knew God personally, because God **walked** in the
garden of Eden:

> Then they heard the [ᴸ sound of the] LORD **God walking** in
> **the garden** during the cool part of the day, and the man and
> his wife hid from the LORD God among the trees in the
> garden. ⁹ But the LORD God called to the man and said,
> "Where are you?" **[Genesis 3:8-9]**

4.) Adam loved God; we don't even have a clue, how Adam
really looked like; how perfect and intelligent he was or how
pure his mindset was!

5.)After eating the fruit, he remain the same, he wasn't
possessed by evil or the spirit of accuser, rather he started to
seeing and feeling "good and evil". Scripture says **[Genesis
3:22]:**

> ²² Then the LORD **God said, "Humans have become like**
> **one of us** [ᶜ referring to the supernatural heavenly
> beings, God and the angels]; **they know good and evil.**
> We must keep them from [ᴸ putting forth their hand and taking
> and] eating some of the fruit from the tree of life, **or they will**
> **live forever."**

Do you see? Scripture says that feeling and seeing "good and
evil" was part of Elohim and Angels; it doesn't mean that God is
evil!

There's no evil in God! [Psalm 92:15; 1 John 1:15]
So, it's always about **the attitude of Heart!**

> Then God said to ·the man [or Adam; 1:27], "You **listened** to
> what your wife said, and you ate fruit from the tree from which
> I commanded you not to eat."

Some translations say: "hearkened the **voice** of thy wife
[DRA]"; "listened to the **voice** of your wife **[ESV]"**; "obeyed

the **voice** of thy wife **[GNV]"**

And Adam's only mistake was to **trust** and <u>listen</u> to a woman more than Lord God! In one word: loving woman more.
Why shouldn't he? There was no **sin** to protect from, and he was unaware of **envy** and **pride**.

Fear came into the world through **disobedience** to God **through guilt!** **Fear** always **separates** man and woman from God. We have to overcome fear in every field.

Things haven't changed; men still **listen** to women more than Lord God, in general, because **we love them so much**! Unfortunately, more than God (it has to change!)! More than ourselves and we honor them **as a weaker vessel [1 Peter 3:7]** Sometimes more than our lives, because they are our "missing rib", **[Genesis 2:22-23]** <u>part our DNA</u>.
And the devil knows that, and he uses women's **ambition** and **seduction** and **envy** to **control** men.
One of the <u>manipulative weapons is **sex**</u>: <u>**sex** is meant to be a blessing</u>, but at the same time, it's <u>destructive</u>.
Women have the power to turn a man against God!
"<u>**Sex sells**</u>" is no longer news nowadays.

And that's why God made man to be "**head of a woman**." And the "**head of a man**" is Christ! **[1 Corinthians 11:3; Ephesians 5:23]**
Not only disobedience to God, but loving woman more than God brought **curse** and the "**Fall**"!
That is the **curse** of the **fallen world**, but **in Christ**, it breaks **if** a woman **submits to man**. That's the **principles** and the **law**.
Man may come to God through Jesus to restore the relationship that Adam had.

<u>Man and women are never equal!</u>
They never meant to be! They were mean to complete each

other! *To become ONE.*
A better question is: *why do we even compare women and men?*
*They are entirely different humans, with entirely different **roles.** **We even can't compare roles.***
*For example, a **knife** and **fork** – they work together, but they don't replace each other. The blade is for cutting, but you can't cut with the fork.*

Why does the world contrast them? Because of the devil. This way of thinking and twisted understanding comes from a fallen world!
*Our mindset has to be renewed **[Ephesians 4:23]***

*To pour little oil to the fire, Paul said how women will be saved **[1 Timothy 2:15]:***

> **15 But** *she will be **saved through having children** [or motherhood; C less likely, a reference to the birth of Christ] if she **continues in faith**, **love**, and **holiness**, with ·**self-control** [propriety; good sense].*

And that's it! *That simple for women! The dissatisfaction comes from the enemy!*

One more thing: *if the bible says and talks **about men**, it doesn't apply automatically to women! Bible can make a difference between man and woman! That's **men's** world! But if we refer **[Galatians 3:28]**:*

> **28 In Christ**, *there is no difference between Jew and Greek [L neither Jew nor Greek], slave and free person, male and female. You are all the same [or united; L one] **in Christ Jesus.***

That is the "powerful scripture," which pastors like to use as an

argument to praise women or to support women. *But there's a misunderstanding: the phrase "**In Christ**" means as in the* **FAITH, literally:** *The* **Faith** *doesn't have* **gender** *nor* **nationality nor slave!**
Faith *is* **Spiritual!**
Paul speaks about **the Faith** *[Galatians 3:23; 26-27]:*

> [23] *Before* **this faith came,** *we were all held prisoners by the law. We had no freedom [were locked up] until God showed us the* **way of faith that** *was coming [┴ the* **coming faith** *would be revealed].*

> [26] *[┴ For] You are all children of God* **through faith in Christ Jesus** *[or In Christ Jesus you are all children/**sons of God through faith**].* [27] *[┴ For] All of you who were baptized **into Christ** have clothed yourselves **with Christ.***

*Back to the position of "**pastor**" (**teacher**):*
A pastor *is a* **teacher** *who* **teaches** *the* **Word of God,** *the* **Spiritual things!**

> „**Not many of you should become teachers,** *my brothers, for you know that* **we who teach will be judged with greater strictness.**" *[James 3:1 ESV]*

The bible doesn't say that women can't spread the gospel, give a testimony, prophesy, heal people, and worship the Lord God in the church and congregations, or teach each other. So, what's going on?
*I call it "**Spiritual ambitions.**" Yes, it does exist.*
Women cannot use the excuse that there are no men anymore, who could be pastors; they won't rise if women won't do their part – **encourage** *and be patient and* **obey.** *The Holy Spirit will*

lift **if it's needed!** Our thoughts aren't God's thoughts and Will:

> The LORD says, **"My thoughts** are not like your **thoughts**.
>   **Your ways** are not like **my ways**.
> [9] Just as the heavens are higher than the earth,
>   so are **my ways higher than your ways**
>   and **my thoughts higher than your thoughts** [Ps. 103:11].

I have seen so many times that women are more "**spiritual ambitions**" than men. And want to run ahead from God's plan and Will:" If men don't take control, then we will."

And **YES** – I'm not tired of repeating myself: Adam was held responsible in the Fall in Eden. **Adam did fail (in a "bigger picture")! [Romans 5:12]:**

> [L Therefore, just as] **Sin came into the world** ·because of what **one man [Adam]** did [L through one man], and **with sin came death.** This is why [L ...and so; or and in this way] **everyone must die** [death spread/passed to all people]—because **everyone sinned**.

The man is the head of the family; he always is responsible, even if the wife makes mistakes, **man will be held accountable**. That's the **Spiritual law**.

But **Salvation** is in **Christ** as the "**Last Adam**":

> [45] [L So also] It is written in the Scriptures: "The **first man, Adam**, became a living ·person [soul; Gen. 2:7]." But the **last Adam** [C Christ] became **a spirit that gives life**.

We have to speak things like they are; about **real reasons**, and **explain** them, and answer to the question "Why" and many pastors are failed to do that and should repent.

> *So, my question is: "How women could even listen to men if the men are already failures from the beginning?"*
> **It's the subconscious mindset.**
> *That is why Satan <u>hates</u> the most the "<u>Book of Genesis</u>" and the "<u>Book of Revelation</u>":*
> *How all started, the "root cause" and the End, how evil will end.*

> *I was gone for about five years without congregation and church! And I returned, and I know that there's work to be done. It's interesting; we tried other congregations, but for some reason, they didn't accept us; they knew us very well. Maybe they considered us traitors and disloyal when I talked about my home congregation, but I assumed that they already knew. They didn't.*

When I got back from Otepää, I told Maila about the conversation that we had with Anre, and it had never disappeared what I **revealed** to another pastor when we were leaving our congregation. Maila said that she had not forgotten it and reminding herself of it all the time.

I asked, *"Why didn't you say anything?!"*

She replied: *"I wanted you to understand by yourself so that the Holy Spirit may reveal it, and if necessary, then I just confirm and agree."*

> *The forgotten things have not vanished, disappeared! We bury them, but they are still there and start to rotten, we may try to deny and forget, but it doesn't mean that they aren't there anymore. And even more, we try to make them little things, make faces that "it's nothing big." And in time, we think that it doesn't matter **anymore**, but its deception.*

I called my Pastor and asked if I could visit him. I will visit him tomorrow.

> *I knew exactly what I have to do – I had to confess and ask forgiveness. It's not an easy thing to do, but I knew that there's no turning back, it's part of **real** Repentance – I must make it right as much as possible. Some damage can't be restored, but we have to do our part so that Lord God could make His! All our actions are installed in the Spirit world: that's where the enemy has the Authority to come in.*

I **confessed** to my father that the Holy Spirit had shown and revealed through His grace that I had lived my whole life in **dishonoring him**: when I was a child and mother provoked against and said all the time to *"piss off."* – From that grew out a certain way of thinking, mindset, and heart attitude. - *"Who do you think you are? Nobody! You just want to play "daddy"."* I wasn't even aware; it just came subconsciously, I was like programmed this way.

I see from my own son that he doesn't honor me, but I demand respect from him, and I'm not some kind of friend, I am a father! It opened my eyes.

My father applauded and said that I am now "**RELEASED**" and "**EVERYTHING I ASK, I SHALL GET**" that there are no more obstacles! He was thrilled that I confessed something like that. That is *a testimony!*

> *I was born when my parents were so young; my mother just turned to 18 and father 19.*
>
> *They become parents too young; father was Christian and mother just turned to God, but my mother was a young rebel against my father because she didn't bear "the Spirit of my father" You may ask a "the Spirit of my father"? Of course, the Spirit of God! The head of a woman is the man!* **[1 Corinthians 11:3; Ephesians 5:23]** *It means that wife doesn't submit to husband* **[Ephesians 5:22-24].** *My mother started to agitate me against my father so that my father might be wrong, and "two against one always wins" and always put to the test my fathers*

> and Lord God's relationship by provoking and manipulating, etc. This Spiritual war lasted years. For today, **they are married the third time, my father's fourth time.** Eventually, they make-up/reconcile, according to the scripture **[1 Corinthians 7:11]**, and grow together as one: "Can't live with her/him and can't live without him/her."
> **My parents are the best example of reconciliation and reunion as Christians, proof that everything is possible!**
> **So, don't you dare to say that marriage cannot be saved!**

In the evening, my father said that he told his friend about my confession. And that friend said that if I NOW turn away, then my consequences will be fatal. I replied that **"I know the price!"**
But I must be honest; it's not like any pressure or some heavy burden – **It's breathing and joy!**

> One thing that I have learned (yes, painful lessons) is that **"don't kill the messenger!"**
> What does it mean? If somebody you know or don't just tells you something hurtful or offensive or has some critical "word" for you, we automatically take a defensive position, and we don't analyze the message.
> Sometime Lord God uses whomever He wants to bring the message, doesn't even matter what we think about that person, does he even have a right to say something or not.
> Most important is what we do with the message, what's the purpose? We take it so personally right away, but maybe there's truth in it? Do we learn? How do we let us effect by the message? Sometimes measures don't matter to save your soul.
> I remember the Balaam's Donkey **[Numbers 22:22-34]**, who spoke. If the donkey speaks to you, it's humiliating, shows how stubborn we could be.
> Like I said; it doesn't matter who's the messenger, even worse; it doesn't matter how he/she talks, offensively or arrogantly, etc.
> – Important is how we react and do we take it into our heart or not. We have to guard our hearts, but sometimes we need to

get rid of our ego. That is her/his problem how he/she speaks, the attitude.
Let us not be affected by other people and not get angry.

Even the bible says [Proverbs 16:32 NRSV]:

*"One who is slow to **anger** is better than the **mighty**, and one whose **temper** is **controlled** than one <u>who captures a city</u>."*

22 NOVEMBER   REPENTANCE AND FORGIVENESS

I visited my pastor and told him everything I had gone through. Also, about my experiences when I started to repent, and that seems to be a journey.

I asked **forgiveness** on the bridge by the beach where he lives; I explained how I **betrayed** him and why I did it so that I could win the Pastor's favor, and then he takes us to his church. And I admitted that was nothing more than just a disappointment.

My Pastor replied: "*I forgive you, and I will set you free from all chains, etc.*"

*In fact, the words that Pastor spoke were much more and much deeper, much more precious than I would have ever thought. I didn't believe that the Pastor would react like that, but I knew I had to do it, and Lord God gave me the **courage**, to be honest – I didn't have any other options, I couldn't put my head under the sand anymore. I'd rather say that my head was under the sand too long, and I had to get up, even if I will be beaten up!*
***The heart** is **important**! <u>It doesn't even matter how people react; the important thing is that you speak what is in the HEART and ask for forgiveness!</u>*
*The **secret of Faith** is in a **pure consciousness**! [1 Timothy 3:9]*

I said: *"You see? Now I understand why I couldn't lead young men's ministry that I proposed to pastor a few years back!"*
The Pastor smiled and said, *"You know, I have a mobile reminder every day that young men's ministry is needed! "*

> My heart has been burning for years for the young men's ministry. I see that men (age between 18-30) need courage, and they need to stand and wake up! Churches are empty of men, or they are passive because of women's activity.

23 NOVEMBER   LIBERATION

The words that the pastor and father said are worth more than gold; they are testimonies of **power** and **mind**! Priceless.

It was a powerful and immense feeling of liberation that cannot be put into words!

24 NOVEMBER

He is **ABBA**, not only **God** – much more personal! He is ADONAI-ELOHIM and ABBA the Father.
We need the **faith of a child; believe like a child!**

> We need that faith, which is **pure** and **sincere**. We have lost it; we make and think that faith is complicated and hard. No, it's not. Our way of thinking is poisoned from our experiences and doubts.
> We have to have a **belief of a child**, but not being **childish**. Also, we must not take the **sincere and pure faith from** our children! We underestimate it.
> Jesus said that we have to **become like a child**, then we will heritage the Kingdom of Heaven!

> "Then he said, "I tell you the truth, you **must change** [or **turn from your sins**; convert; ᴸturn] and become **like little children**. Otherwise, you will never enter the kingdom of heaven. ⁴ The greatest person in the kingdom of heaven [ᴸtherefore] is the one who makes **himself humble** [and becomes] like **this [little] child**." **[Matthew 18:3]**

The faith of a child is stolen; that's the **main reason of our disbelief, lack of faith.**
We are **afraid** to believe like a child. And our pure and simple understanding of Christ is ruined.

> "But I am afraid that **your minds will be led away** [or corrupted] **from your true [sincere] and pure following of Christ** just as Eve was tricked [deceived] by the snake [serpent] with his evil ways [cunning; craftiness; Gen. 3:1–6]. **[2 Corinthians 11:3]**

I've seen it so clearly in my own children. For example:
if you offer them candy, they always say: "**yes and yes and yes!**" And that's it.
But if somebody offers us "candy," then our first thought is "**Why**?" **Where's the "catch"?** We **suspect** - **children believe and trust**. Yes, when they grow, their pure, sincere thinking will also decrease in time. So, we doubt everything.
And it's maybe hard to understand, but "**simplicity is the key**".
And we have to admit that we don't have that faith, even as a small mustard seed:

> Jesus answered, "Because **your faith is too small** [you have **so little faith**]. I tell you **the truth**, if your faith is as big as [as small as; the size of; ᴸas; like] a mustard seed, you can say to this mountain, 'Move from here to there,' and it will move. All things will be possible [ᴸNothing would be impossible] for you. **[Matthew 17:20-21]**

*Jesus **rebuked** us for **unbelief**.*

> [5] *The apostles said to the Lord, "Give us **more faith**!"*
> [6] *The Lord said, "If **your faith** were the size of a mustard seed, you could say to this mulberry tree, 'Dig yourself up [Be uprooted] and plant yourself in the sea,' and it would **obey you**. [Luke 17:5-6]*

25 NOVEMBER

All things come at once - Maila needs to study for an exam, she has two of them, I need to study "SCRUM". Now I have to choose which one has to learn, which one is more important: Maila's hairdresser's exam or my "SCRUM" test! We must not give up! Maila must graduate from the hairdresser's school.

> *Maila graduated the hairdresser's school as the best in her group. Glory to God!*

26 NOVEMBER

Looking back at the time when I was working, the question arises in my heart: *"Is that ALL?"*
I **really** want more!
I know that I am called as the **GIVER [2 Corinthians 9:8-14]: it's even a ministry/service.** I know it when I was a teenager that I have the Giver's heart.

27 NOVEMBER

On Thursday, the Superena max jackpot is 325 million
ABBA is a miracle worker!

Does **Jesus testify of us before ABBA**? **[Matthew 10:32; Luke 12:8]**
He is the **helper [counselor; advocate (Romans 8:34)] in the presence of the Father [1 John 2:1-2]**

It is written **[Romans 8:15]**:

> *"The Spirit you received does not make you **slaves again to fear** [or You did not receive the spirit of slavery, leading to fear]; instead, you received the Spirit · who **adopts you as God's children** [L of adoption]. ·With [Through] that Spirit we cry out, "**ABBA** [C Aramaic for "Father"; Mark 14:36], **Father**."*

> *We talk so much about "fear", and still, we can't draw a line between "Fear" and "fear". Some people may say that "fear" can be useful; it can keep you alive. Yes - in some circumstances, for example, "fear of death". It can void death, and at the same time, it can make you panic, and you don't know where to run to get help, often it's the wrong place. But as a Christian, we don't afraid death; at least, we shouldn't.*
> *"**fear**"- comes from the fallen world; there are many reasons why we afraid, evil uses it to control people, etc. Everybody knows the meaning of "fear."*
> *"**Fear**"– comes from respect and deference; Fear of God is all different things, and the motive is good, like a father with his child, that child may trust him in all things, and it consists **trust** and **love**. It's so much more profound, "Fear of God" sets us*

free, free from twisted minds and wrong motives; world "fear" makes your prisoner and controlled by, makes you anxious, etc.

"18 ·Where **God's love is, there is no fear** [L *There is no fear in love*], because **God's perfect love drives out fear** [T *perfect love casts out fear*]. It is **punishment that makes a person fear, so love is not made perfect [complete] in the person who fears** [C *fear of punishment, not an appropriate fear of God; compare* Prov. 1:7; 2 Cor. 7:15; Phil. 2:12*].*" **[1 John 4:18]**

*"**Fear of sinning**". We are so afraid that everything that we do – is sin!*
The enemy keeps us sinning and tells us how great and powerful sin is, and you will never be cleansed of it, and you are doomed! That you're meaningless.
That has been very convincing, and it keeps us under his control.
But it's so wrong!
*For example, **[Ephesians 4:26]**: Anger; you may get angry, but you may not stay in it and keep it inside so that it may grow. You have to control **it**, not that **it** controls you!*

*"Be **angry** and do not **sin**.[a] Don't let the sun go down on your anger,"*

All mistakes aren't **sin**, but they can become one!
We are no longer **slaves of sin [Romans 6:22]**

Like David prayed for forgiveness from God, saying that he sinned against God only, and only against Him! **[Psalm 51:4 NIV]**

*"Against **you, you only**, have **I sinned** and done what is **evil in your sight**; so you are right in your verdict and justified when you judge."*

*And David prayed for the **new pure heart** [Psalm 51:12], and David knew what he was asking for. Why don't we?*

*__Fear of God__, as **godliness** will keep us from sinning! And we have to admit that we are losing godliness, Fear of God, and we use to enjoy "**Christianity**" and God's Love, without reminding ourselves that **He is Holy** and with **Holy Wrath, Consuming Fire [Hebrews 12:29]**. It means that we take the good out of the bible and ignore all the evil and **strict**, all the punishment, and build our faith in specific motivating scriptures, and we take it out of context. I call it "**hedonistic Christianity**." And we ignore our sin, and we consider ourselves holy and sinless, or we just reject responsibility to God and say, "He will do as He pleases." And we let **fate** lead us. And we **use** God as the "Coca-Cola machine" to pick what we want. After all, we say: "God will make things right" and then be at **peace** with yourself and say that God gave that **peace**. Again, there's a deceiving understanding of "__peace__" or "__Peace__."*

*"__peace__"- is from the world, it means that you just keep telling yourself that everything is ok and you are starting to ignore and become cold, you will not care anymore eventually. It's the devil's work- he wants you to stay in your bubble and be **lukewarm** and don't understand the world we live in.*

"__Peace__" is from God, and it is He: the Holy Spirit: Holy Spirit in us gives Peace by knowing that He leads us and provides wisdom to stand and fight our fights.

***There's no Peace** without the Holy Spirit!*

*[26] But the **Advocate, the Holy Spirit, whom** the Father **will send** in my name, will teach you all things and will remind you of everything I have said to you. [27] **Peace** I leave with you; **my peace I give you**. I do not give to you **as the world gives**. Do not let your hearts be troubled and do not be afraid. **[John 14:26-27 NIV]***

We need to find the middle path between these extremes, the narrow road. Even Jesus said so:

*"**Enter through the narrow gate**. [ᴸ Because] The **gate is wide** and the **road is wide** [broad; spacious; or easy] that leads to **hell** [ᴸ destruction; ruin], and many people enter through that gate. ¹⁴ But the **gate is small** and the **road is narrow [or difficult; hard]** that leads to true life. Only a few people [And there are few who] find that road. **[Matthew 7:13-14]***

*Again, there's a difference between "**fate**" and "**destiny**."*
*"**fate**"- forsaken by God; for the **world**, for **unbelievers, who has renounce God,** and those who are **lukewarm**, so that all spirits, demons could lead them, use them on their behalf, being a tool for every spirit and demon, etc. Some people call it "luck"*

*"But as **for you who ·left** [abandoned; forsook] **the Lᴏʀᴅ**,*
    who forgot about my holy mountain,
*who **·worship the god Luck** [ᴸ spread a table for Fortune/Luck; ᶜ Hebrew Gad, a pagan god],*
    *·who hold religious feasts for the **god Fate** [ᴸ fill bowls of mixed wine for Fate; ᶜ Hebrew Meni, a pagan god],*
*¹² I ·decide your fate, and **I will punish you** with my sword [ᴸ destine/number you for the sword].*
    ***You will all ·be killed** [fall in the slaughter; or bow to the executioner],*
because I called you, but you refused to answer.
    I spoke to you, but you wouldn't listen.
*You did ·the things I said were **evil** [ᴸ evil before my eyes] and **chose to do things ·that displease me** [ᴸ I did not delight in]." **[Isaiah 65:11-12]***

*"**destiny**" comes from "**Destination**"- better word is "**Purpose**"; is **God's Will, His best plan,** and the specific **calling** in your*

life, which you have to **fight** for yourself, the **track** on the **race**, the **path** of the **chosen**. But it's our choice to make, **free will** to **choose Jesus or the world**.

> "**Strive** to **enter** through the **narrow door**. For **many**, I tell you, will <u>seek to enter</u> and will **not be able**." **[Luke 12:24]**

"**Once saved; always saved" is a deception** that can't handle criticism.

Good news! I know that's nothing new, but the good news is that we don't have to sin **anymore;** we have to become perfect **[Matthew 5:48; Matthew 19:21]**! <u>Everybody **has sinned** **[Romans 3:23]**,</u> That's the message from Paul and Jesus. John says it without illustration **[1 John 3:5-6]:**

> "**5** But you know that he appeared so that he **might take away our sins**. And **in him is no sin. 6 No one who lives in him keeps on sinning**. No one who **continues** to **sin** has either **seen him** or **known** him."

John makes it really easy and straightforward to understand **[1 John 3:8-10]:**

> "**8 The one who does what is sinful is of the devil**, because the devil has been sinning from the beginning. The reason the Son of God appeared was to destroy the **devil's work. 9 No one** who is **born of God** will **continue to sin**, because **God's seed** remains in them; **they cannot go on sinning**, because they have **been born of God. 10** This is how we know who the **children of God** are and who the **children of the devil** are: Anyone who does not do **what is right is not God's child**, nor is anyone who does not love their brother and sister."

John says that by the sin we are defined as *"**children of God**"* or *"**children of the devil**"*
And it's true: if your reborn in Christ and baptized in the Holy Spirit, you will see the sin more and more clearly, and it makes you *"**spiritually sick**."*

So there's no excuse for sinning and say that *"**nobody's perfect**."* You may say that I'm not **yet** perfect, but **I am "work in progress", and I'm on the way!** That's an attitude of the heart.

> *"**I will forgive them** for [be merciful with regard to] the **wicked** things they **did** [their unrighteousness/wickedness],*
> *and **I will not remember their sins anymore** [Jer. 31:31–34; Luke 22:20]."**[Hebrews 8:12]***

28 NOVEMBER

GIVER

So many times, I've heard from Christians that they have experience with *"wrong giving's."* And you need to be a *"Smart Giver"* not being an *"A stone to stumble over."*
But I do not agree, but I believe that's always about your **motives and heart attitude because God loves a cheerful giver [2 Corinthians 9:7]**

> *Yes, **they can mishandle money**, and **we regret giving them money, but it's not our decision to make what they do with it or judge or make conclusions!** Jesus never did. And if we do this, we will close all the doors to give, and our negative experiences bring forth disappointments.*
> ***Giving is not conditional.***

> Also, we should not make **slaves** and **debtors.**
> It's an important topic, and I will not go deep, but I prefer separating the "**giver**" and the "**sower.**"

Yesterday, on Wednesday, when I bought the Superena max lottery, I felt that it was not the end - so strange, there's something else...

Superena max jackpot is 500 million €! It's never been so high - it's no coincidence!
I also got the numbers, the vision of winning numbers yesterday! That was the feeling!

We decided to fast with Maila for two days!

The power of the Sacrificial Blood of Jesus! That is the revelation! And also the *"Power of the Resurrection."*
I want that mustard seed Faith; I demand that faith, I shout and roar and cry for that FAITH!
I want to receive a **Heart** that worships Father The ABBA!

A few days ago, talking about the testimonies of repentance to a friend, who recently visited us, my father said that I must not become a victim of *"pride of life/possessions."* **[1 John 2:16 EXB]**
Maybe a better word is: "***worldly arrogance***" **[1John 2:16 ISV]**
I have experiences that "*wisdom of the world*" makes your ego grow, your self-awareness and pride, but "*wisdom of the God*" makes you humble: because you know that it's not coming from me, it is from the Holy Spirit! He just gives how He pleases, gives and takes if needed.
These two are opposites of each other.
"*wisdom of the world*" can be learned; you just need a good memory and ambition;

"*Wisdom of the God*" comes from the Holy Spirit.
"*God has made the wisdom of the world foolish.*" **[1 Corinthians 1:18-30; 1 Corinthians 3:18-20]**
Also James compared the "*wisdom of the world*" and "*wisdom of the God*" **[James 3:13-18]**:

> *Are there those among you who are **truly wise** and ·**understanding** [insightful; discerning]? Then they should show it by ·**living right** [their good life/conduct/lifestyle] and ·**doing good things** [their deeds/works] with a ·**gentleness** [humility; meekness; Matt. 5:5; 11:29; Gal. 6:1] that comes from wisdom.* ¹⁴ *But **if you have bitter ·jealousy** [or envy] **and ·are selfish** [have selfish ambition] **in your hearts, do not ·brag** [boast; Jer. 9:23–24]. **Your ·bragging** [boasting] **is a lie ·that hides** [that denies; ᴸ against] **the truth** [or Don't cover up the truth with bragging or lying].* ¹⁵ ***That kind of "wisdom" does not come ·from God*** *[ᴸ down from above; ᶜ that is, from heaven] **but ·from the world** [is earthly]. **It is ·not spiritual** [natural; "soulish"; ᶜ human life apart from God; 1 Cor. 2:14]; **it is ·from the devil** [demonic].* ¹⁶ ***Where ·jealousy*** *[or envy] **and ·selfishness** [selfish ambition] **are, there will be ·confusion** [chaos; disorder] **and every ·kind of evil** [evil thing/practice].* ¹⁷ *But **the wisdom that comes from ·God** [ᴸ above; 3:15] **is first of all pure, then peaceful** [peace-loving], **gentle** [patient; considerate], and ·**easy to please** [or willing to yield; or open to reason]. **This wisdom is ·always ready to help those who are troubled and to do good for others** [ᴸ full of mercy and good fruits]. **It is ·always fair** [impartial] **and ·honest** [sincere; unhypocritical].*

"*Everyone who has been **given much**, much will be demanded/required!*" **[Luke 12:48 EXB]** there is a **great responsibility**!" Sometimes I ask myself if the price is too high, and I cannot handle more; it turns into a burden. But then I realize that is not mine to carry, I myself can't – but with Lord God…

I **repent** of *"pride of life/possessions"* as *"**worldly arrogance.**"*
I don't consider myself smarter or better in any way.
Also the *"**lust of the flesh**"* and *"**lust of the eyes**"* **[1 John 2:16]**.

> *"Stop **loving the world** and the **things that are in the world**. If anyone persists in loving the world, the Father's love is not in him." **[1 John 2:15 ISV]***
> *It means that we all do that, all the **passion** and **lust** and **enjoyment**; I know that's hard, but we can grow in it: **grow to the mindset of Jesus**!*
> *These things of this world make us **slaves of addictions** and pull us even more in-depth, so that we may forget that's only a **temporary world.***
> *I pray that Lord God may open your eyes to see that's not all; the world we live in is not all; there's a much bigger world waiting for us!*

I want to walk in the *LIGHT*, not to love this world. I believe I have done it a lot!

We, as Christians, are "**worldly arrogance**."
First, I thought that we are just egoists, and it's all about our mindset, but it's not only about that. **Mindset** begins from **Heart attitude**!
We are so misled!
We are the stewards of the mysteries of God **[1 Corinthians 4:1 ASV]** – This also makes us arrogant, pride, subconsciously makes us better than other Christians, brothers, sisters.
No, it should make us very careful and know that it comes with responsibility.

> *That's a harsh statement from me-but we must end the competition between who is the better Christian or compare each other! It's our Heart attitude! We don't say it aloud, but these are our thoughts of heart, for example: "I'm not as sinful*

like the other, and he/she even dares to call himself/herself as Christian! What a disgrace!"
We need to grow in Agape Love! Also, Disciples made the same mistakes, let us not! **[Luke 22:24-27; Luke 9:46-48]**
The same thing is with "**envy**"; we are <u>jealous</u> of each other if some "brother in Christ" lives better than others. It is called "**religious face**" or "**Holy face**" We don't really know the whole story, it could be deceiving. It usually is.
Like I already said: Let us not forget that we have **our <u>own</u> race to win! <u>We don't compete with others</u>! Never meant to!**
Like Paul said **[Hebrews 12:1]:**

[EXB] ... let us run the **race that is before us** and **never give up** [with endurance/perseverance]. We should [Let us] remove from our lives [get rid of; cast aside] **anything** that would get in the way [impedes/hinders us] and the **sin** that so easily ·**holds us back** [entangles/clings to us].

[ISV] ... throwing off **everything** that **hinders** us and especially the **sin** that so easily **entangles** us, let us **keep running with endurance** the **race set before us.**

500 million € Superena Max today!

Maila and I fasted, Maila had two exams, and she passed these! Hallelujah!

We fasted until 9 pm.

Before I went to bed, I checked the results, and we didn't win Superena Max jackpot.
The Holy Spirit asked:" What should you do now, and what would you decide: Will you give up and never fast again and stop

*seeking the Kingdom of God **[Matthew 6:33]** in the mornings?*
I replied: *"I have nowhere to go, and I want to continue!"*

---

*This is the moment: "**how seriously do you want me?**" Are you willing to give up for 500 million €? It's still a question in a practical situation. **The decision** is already made, and there's no turning back without consequences! Are there any doubts about the decision?*

*That's our world problem: we change our decision overnight and take no responsibility for our actions. Its cowardliness! I remind you that cowards will burn in **hell [Revelation 21:8]***

<u>*That's **my** quote*</u>: **"God hates cowards who fear to believe!"**
*It doesn't mean that I don't fear or that I'm no **coward** in some things, but I acknowledge it, and I'm eager to grow in it and become fearless. **Fearless** doesn't mean **mindless**!*

---

1 DECEMBER

I've discovered that now the Superena Max jackpot is 587 million €! That's a record!

We decided with Maila that it is nonsense, such as fooling and time stretching, and yet not received the jackpot!

But - *"To Be or Not to Be!"* We believe!

During the day as I prayed, some things came to my heart:

1.) **Decision** – Do we give up if we don't win?

2.) **Fear** – Fear is caused by comparing ourselves to others and their situations. For example, Christians who had *"private bankruptcy."*

Is that the **Will of God**? How will Lord God be **glorified**?

Fear and fright, and the panic have me if I don't win, knowing that the enemy will get what he wants. And my greatest **fear** is being fulfilled, and I'm a failure!

"Negative faith" is produced by fear and doubt; and fear of failure!

"Unbelief" and *"Negative faith"* *(bad faith)* are two different things; one is passive, lukewarm, and the other has a power that the worst will fulfill, like "worrying". And it does because fear is a very powerful thing. "Negative faith" may bring a curse upon by opening the door of the spirit world.

"Negative faith" produces negative thinking and negative words, and we know where they will lead us: these are all connected.

For example, "worrying" and negative words: it has a destructive impact on your soul and mind. My grandmother "Y" is the "master of worrying", and everything about she worried about, were fulfilled! And that mindset and "faith" will grow!

Even Jesus says that we shouldn't worry, and worrying, can't add an hour to your life **[Luke 12:25]**, but **it may take it**.

We are mistaken if we think that "worrying" and "carrying" are synonyms: it doesn't mean if you don't **worry**, you don't **care!** There's antonym called *"careful."*

At the same time, the Holy Spirit made it clear that such fooling and obstructing aren't from the enemy; it's because of me; will I stay and fight to the end, will I receive the Kingdom of God or not and **will I give away the fear**!

I talked about it with Maila, and we prayed together.

Also, *conclusion:* We don't know the Love of Lord God, we have forgotten it, or Lord God hasn't yet revealed it. Otherwise, there would not be a **fear**, but we would know that ABBA the Father **really** gives the Best and that He loves us, and we would trust Him! I know that I have forgotten, and I have a very wrong understanding of the word *"love."*

---

*Even right now, there's only one word for "love" in English, but in Ancient Greek, there were **eight different** meanings of "love":*
*1.) **Eros** – sexual passion: for the opposite sex.*

2.) **Philia** – *friendship*

3.) **Ludus** – *playful love*

4.) **Agape**- *love for everyone (**Lord God's love**)*

5.) **Pragma** – *longstanding love: marriage needs it to last and to avoid divorce.*

6.) **Philautia** – *a love of the self: unhealthy variety associated with narcissism and focused on personal fame and fortune.*

7.) **Storge** – *family love: between family members, protective and kinship-based love, also patriotic toward country or the same team.*

8.) **Mania** – *obsessive love*

I don't want to go deep, but we misuse the word "love", and the true meaning just fades away.

For example: "I love my car" or "I love that food" or "I love my wife" or "I love God."

"Love is expressed in women in the sense of security, and in men with respect, which fosters dignity."

---

2 DECEMBER	DREAM and REPENTANCE

I had a dream about my ex-girlfriend "**K**":

*"**K**" divorced from her husband and became a legal caregiver to her grandfather, who was unable to walk.*

Then she looked for me and called me to her place to search for comfort. I saw that she was full of bitterness and arrogance, and I told it to her.

She said: "Just like my husband- same words. Now go away!"

I replied: "With my pleasure, but demons influence you, and you are trapped!"

She asked: "How?"

> *I replied:" You are being affected by your grandfather!"*
> *Then she admitted that her grandfather is still having fun with*
> *women and can't be satisfied.*
> *Then I said: "You see; it's the spirit of fornication!"*
> *She understood, and I said that she must* **make up / reconcile**
> *with her husband! And if needed, I may support her during the*
> *process."*

When I woke up after dreaming, the question started to bother me:
"Why I still see only her ("K") in my dreams, time after time?"
When I saw her on the second of November, a strange feeling hit
me - *"Repressed feelings are not lost feelings."*
And I knew right away that when I'm rich, she could be my
"stumbling rock." And I have to give it to the Lord God!
I don't want to be like a Solomon, who fell not because he was the
richest man in the world, but he fell because of the deception of
his wives and concubines.

Conclusion: **I repented of:**
1.) Fear of comparing myself with other Christians and brothers in
Christ.
2.) I made a **DECISION** that I will follow the Lord God forever; the
only prayer was: that I would be hot and **fervent**, full of the fire of
the Holy Spirit: where ever I go or do!
I refuse to be lukewarm!
3.) Gave "K" as my *"stumbling rock"* to ABBA the Father; from a
deeply deceptive heart.

As I've said before, we have *"**Unfinished Stories.**"*

> *I have to say that I'm free from these relationships, I don't bear*
> *some "hidden love" inside my deepest heart. Yes – they have*
> *been a part of my life, just one phase in a longer journey. I could*
> *talk to them freely about everything, and if necessary: do some*
> *explanations. I'm not afraid to communicate and keep touch*
> *with them, if it's needed.*

I promised and swore that I will never cheat on Maila!
Physically - I rather die!
We capture every thought and make it obey Christ. **[2 Corinthians 10:5-6]**

3 DECEMBER

587 million €
We did not win it, raises many questions. Mainly disappointing because we believed and declared "together in unity through the Sacrificial Blood of Jesus" but nothing.
It causes sadness.

I feel something happened; I don't know what it is, frustration maybe?

4-5 DECEMBER

I went to IT training to study "SCRUM", and my hope starts to rely on other things, worldly things - the attitude: "*I will do myself then if God doesn't do anything.*"
But I don't give up!

6 DECEMBER

I trust God; some emotion disappeared; in the meantime, I didn't seem to care about anything anymore: and I have to manage and act on my own!

I WANT YOU, JEHOVAH! I want to give my Hear entirely to You, ABBA! We cannot live based on emotions!
When we say that we *"love"* Jesus, but they are feelings/emotions, but if we take them away, do we still *"love"*? **Love** is not an **emotion**; it's a **decision**, and even more!

We are based too much on **feelings** and **emotions**, that's a question: **Who rules?**

Who rules? 1.) Soul 2.) Flesh/Body or 3.) The Spirit? Which is the first?

"Who's driving a car?"

That is my very simple example of "Body/SOUL/SPIRIT" illustration:

"Body/flesh" is a car. It doesn't matter which car, some have better ones, some have faster ones. But I prefer a limousine on this example. Also, you have to maintain and take care of the car.

"Soul" is the You: who is sitting in the back of a limousine, behind the driver's glass, which separates the salon.

You think you know where to go, but the driver knows the way and gives some advice.

Honestly, we don't know the endpoint without guidance.

"Spirit" is the chauffeur (<u>driver</u>): whom you have to trust and where ever he drives. Sometimes the chauffeur (driver) could also be a **bodyguard**.

It's <u>our **free will** to choose, who's the **driver**</u>, but the <u>driver seat is never empty!</u>

It's meant to be for the Holy Spirit **[1 Corinthians 6:19]**, but usually, there's somebody else <u>whom we trust</u> **[1 John 4:1]** and who wants us to be deceived and drive us far from God's Best and Will. Sometimes the Holy Spirit calls you and says that you have the wrong chauffeur (driver); It's your choice whether you listen to Him or not.

<u>There can't be two drivers!</u>

> **"No one can serve two ·masters** [lords]**. The person will hate one master** and **love the other**, or **will ·follow** [be devoted/loyal to] **one master** and **·refuse to follow** [despise] **the other. You cannot serve both God and ·worldly riches** [money; ᴸ mammon]**." [Matthew 6:24]**

We talk so much about **Heavenly Father's** love for us, but we don't talk about "**loving God**";
Do we even love God for **real**?
Jesus said that first commandment is **[Matthew 22:37]**:

> „Jesus answered, "'**Love the Lord** your God with all your **heart, all your soul**, and **all your mind** [Deut. 6:5].'"

What about "loving God"? **[1 John 5:3]**

> „**Loving God means** [L For this is the love of God:] ·**obeying** [keeping] **his commands**. And God's **commands** are not ·too hard [burdensome] for us [Matt. 11:30],"

I have noticed that many say that they **love Jesus**, but they really don't **love God**. It's easier to love Jesus than God himself, easy is to divide them from **Trinity.**
I had a **revelation last year**, that I have never loved God **truly**, I just thought that I did, maybe in some way – in my own way.
But that was a shock for me. I loved an illusion about Jesus, because it was hard to me to love God, who is the same as in **Old Testament – the Lord God with Holy Fire; all the slaughter, etc.,** and He is the same!
But now I do! **Old Testament** and **New Testament God is the same**, and Jesus sacrifice made it all **perfect** and **complete**!
Why I love **Elohim Adonai**?
Very simple: I love because **He** is **Righteous, Faithful, Perfect and that He is "same yesterday, today and tomorrow".**

Today Maila and her friends "T.A" and "K.U" met in the café; nothing is a coincidence.

Maila's friend prayed for Maila, and they had **visions**:
1.) "T. A" saw a vision during prayer that we have the **final "push"** like giving childbirth, just a little bit more…

2.) "K.U" saw in the spirit many baby chicks with their beak open and waiting for the food from the mother.

To be fair: So many have been prophesied to us over the years. And in the end, you just don't believe them anymore, because they haven't fulfilled and become insensitive and you don't care anymore.

Of course, there might be false prophecies, but the right ones you already know! Lord God has previously spoken about it; it has always been inside you, just these prophecies are confirmations, especially when they are the same prophecies from different people!

*These days there are so many **false prophets**, and we have to be careful and see the motives of these so-called "prophecies." Even **Jesus warned** us about **false prophets [Matthew 7:15; 24:11,24; Mark 13:22]***

*and said that we would recognize them by the **fruits** [Matthew 7:16-20]*

*But fruits take time, but we **desperately need "Gift of Discernment" [1 Corinthians 12:10]**, so that we may **recognize spirits(demons and evil),** and not be deceived nor accomplice, rather **expose them [Ephesians 5:11 ESV]:***

Take no part in the unfruitful works of darkness, but **instead expose them.**

---

*I see that we don't have it; we **think** that we have and believe it, but we are so easily fooled, and it is **very dangerous.***

*Also, Peter and Paul **warned** us so many times; it means it's dangerous to fall in their deception and bring destructive heresies to church **[2 Peter 2:1-22 ESV]** and do not trust every spirit **[1 John 4:1-6]***

We hurry up to prophecy so quickly, without carrying the responsibility of your words and "prophecy." False prophets were slaughtered in old testament times, but today?

Every day, I give up and slay my *"Lust for the Flesh"*, the *"Lust for the Eyes,"* and the *"Pride of Life"* so that they would stay away from me and won't become part of my flesh until I'm entirely immune!

During repentance, I became free, but now I must remain free and clean! Bring forth the **appropriate fruit of repentance:** *producing the fruit worthy with repentance.* **[Matthew 3:8; Luke 3:8; Apostles 26:20]** *We have to be sober and alert because our adversary the devil is seeking whom he may devour!* **[1 Peter 5:8 BRG]**, *and we must not give him an* **opportunity** *and* **place** *to defeat you!* **[Ephesians 4:27 EXB]**

---

16 DECEMBER   FASTING#1

Purpose of the fasting:
1.) Hear the voice of the Holy Spirit
2.) Pray for My grandfather "H" and grandmother "V" as they will reunite for forgiveness.
3.) Faith and Decision
4.) Sex is prohibited

The first problem that we have is that we don't talk about **sex** *at all: it's so prohibited topic and embarrassing, and it seems that sex is only for making descendants and nothing to enjoy. No, it's so much more: Lord God created it to be perfect between husband and wife; even Solomon wrote a song about enjoying each other!* **[Songs of Solomon 7]** *Sex is meant to be pure, and it's not just some acts in the flesh-it's to* **unite two souls,** *interweaving:* **transaction from the physical world to the spiritual.**

I believe there are no words to describe what happens during that; what energy it releases!

Lord God even made a **system for pregnancy** that you may enjoy each other without getting pregnant. It means that you have control over it, **ovulation calendar**. I know that it's a serious topic, but it's my opinion: yes, the Lord God said that we have to multiply several times in the bible **[Genesis 1:28;9:1]**, but don't forget that when He said it: there wasn't any, literally! Now there are over seven and a half **billion** people!

"Controlling pregnancy" is another topic that I'm not going to talk about because the debate among Christians is huge! Maybe one day!

But devil took something so beautiful and perfect and twisted like he always does, some perverted fornication to disgrace Lord God creating!

<u>As I am honest</u> – I had about five sexual relationships before marriage, and I called myself a Christian!

And all these relationships ended with broken hearts. All of them tore my heart apart! I even tried to commit suicide once (I was about 18 years old.) I ate some drugs and drank alcohol, hoping I would never wake up again. Lord God had another plan with me. Waking up in the morning, it turned out that the drugs "best before date" had ended about a year back. After that, I thought I should get stronger drugs and try again, but something touched my soul, and I knew that the Lord God is real!

It's interesting – My wife Maila just said a few days back when I talked her about heartbreaking relationships:

"I believe that is <u>why breaking-ups and heartbreaks were so serious and hurtful because you had sex with them!</u>"

And it's true – like I mentioned that sex is much more, and <u>every intercourse leaves a mark from the **soul** to another **soul**.</u>

That is why I have regretted for years that I had sex with several women, and I have no experience of being clean and virgin until I get married. I have repented from that regret; otherwise, I couldn't write about that now.

I don't even have to mention that **sex is part of love,** and **part of marriage**, right?

Having sex during fasting is wrong!

I had received a word that during the fasting, I can't have sex! It seems so obvious because we know what fasting is.
I fast from the deeds of *flesh*, and it's fasting from **food**. It's biblical fasting, and it's not fasting about *Facebook*, or *TV* or *internet, etc.* – no. *Flesh* needs to die, and the basis of life is *flesh* – it is needed to survive; and if you take food away, you will see how fast *flesh* will start to scream.
The spirit must dominate, not flesh! So, I cannot be submitted to the flesh, I've stumbled upon it once before and it kind of resets everything, makes it pointless-because one of the ideas of fasting is to cleanse yourself and keep from flesh acts and physical contact. I experienced the consequence on my body: I won't go into details.

Dear Holy Spirit, please speak about why an Authority and Faith don't work? Honestly - without illustration!
I can't grow faith by myself or lift myself from hair!

What will happen to our car?
The leasing company wants the car back because I already behind with my payments.

17 DECEMBER	FASTING#2

The car - What is YOUR WILL, ABBA?
Intervene NOW!
Show that You are the Mighty One I serve!

> *We must be honest with ourselves – even if I could keep my car, some miracle – but still, I don't have money to keep it running; not money for insurance, for fuel, etc.*

> *My father said very brilliant quote: "**honest life is the protection of the soul**"*

18 DECEMBER   FASTING#3

Today I was hit by a high fever.
Getting a fever middle of fasting hits you on the ground.
Why?

Today was also the deadline for returning the car to the leasing
company, but I misread the notification, I hope I won't be charged
for that if I return the car when I feel better.

19 DECEMBER   FASTING#4

As my health was weak, especially during fasting, the fever got
high, and I **promised** to help my mother to transport Jannly
(mother's dog.) Jannly has eyelid surgery, which cannot be
postponed. But I **promised**. But God is AWESOME; He arranged
mother's friend to help her, who lives next door, and is a dog
breeder (we got our first dog from them - Tibetan Mastiff)

> Why is that such a big deal? It's about a word called *"**promise**"*.
> It's not intentional, but I have not kept my promises or have
> delayed them. It's always about our priorities, and I see the
> same pattern everywhere these days. In ancient times, if
> somebody promised, then the **word of man** meant something,
> that was a **respectful thing**, and people **relied** on that. If you
> didn't keep your Word, you had to pay! Today, people don't
> respect and don't take responsibility for their actions; instead of
> that, they make all sorts of excuses. There's a saying: "The fool
> is the one who finds no excuses."
> I don't speak about exceptions, but about the mindset of these
> days, that spreads all over the society. Also, there's a saying:
> "man gives the word, a man takes the word."
> What an attitude! Primarily, I see it in our generation, the older
> generation still knows its meaning.
> So, now nobody cares, they only think:" it's not really a big
> deal!"

> Better not to promise! But I recommend that if we promise, we will keep it seriously and with all our attention and power, so we would not let something break our promise. Lord God sees our Heart and our Heart motives. If we keep and give our best to keep and something wants to steal or come between us, we have to keep it – even if needed, with our lives, but the Lord God is with you!
>
> The same thing applies to Lord God – if you promise something to Him – then do it right away, do not delay to fulfill!
>
> **[Ecclesiastes 5:1-5]**
>
> That's the reason why we have lawyers and notary to make agreements on paper, because we don't keep promises. The basic "excuse" is that "I don't remember that…"
>
> "The man is known for his promises." **Keeping** promises is also an **act**.
>
> I want to grow in this knowledge and repent for that.

I finished my fasting earlier than I expected to regain my strength back so I could fight the fever.

I still prayed and tried to understand where did the fever come from?

My mother started to say that it is definitely the flu – That seriously haven't been sick in five years! I know it's an attack!

I drink a lot of water to cool myself and go to the toilet time after time.

> NB! **No medicine** or antipyretic to reduce fever. **I'm against medications of any kind.**
>
> I was in chronic angina for over ten years, several times in a year, and I know what fever is.

The fever jumps up and down.
Today is worse than yesterday: fever is 39,5 °C (102,2°F), and as
<u>I was awake</u>, I started to see **visions**:

---

*<u>Vision vs Dream:</u> "Dream" is what we see while we are sleeping
in a particular context, and "Vision" is something you see with
your eyes while you're awake. It's like you see two worlds
simultaneously, physical and the spiritual world bonded
together. It's nothing that you can "imagine" - you can't because
it's not coming from **you,** and you know the difference right
away.*

FIRST VISION

*I was in some kind of spaceship that looked like a revolver drum,
full of people and moving in a spiral upwards all the time—moving
higher and higher.*
*It was like another **portal**, stops were made, and people got off, I
reached the end alone, in front of the great throne: The throne
was like inside the cliff, but open from above, everything was dark
and full of stars, a bright light was shining from far behind the
throne.*
*And I saw someone sitting on the throne in the dark, he didn't **say**
a word, but I **knew** what he was **speaking** (It means that he didn't
open his mouth.)*
*Satan tried to deceive me as if I was in the <u>court of Jesus</u>, but it
was so obvious. He thought that the darkness could disguise him
so that I could be fooled because I didn't see his face, just a
shape.*
*I was standing there, and I thought that I would remain silent like
Jesus was when he was crucified – I was in such Peace. He
began to <u>accuse me, to judge over me,</u> and then I realized, and I*

interrupted him, saying: "**NO! JESUS IS THE ONLY ONE WHO JUDGES THE JUDGEMENT, AND YOU WILL BE JUDGED, BUT I AM THE SON OF GOD!**"

Then some powerful, bright "**Light**" was opened from above and like a lasso or something came down and grabbed me and started to pull me up to the "**Light**".

Then the devil jumped down from his throne and tried to grab me from my leg, but he didn't have the strength to hold and pull. I felt that his grip was so weak as a feather.

And I went to the "**Light.**"

Just to clarify: I am a "**son** of God", not the "**SON** of GOD" There's only one **S**ON of GOD, I'm just adopted son.
And **satan is accuser [Revelation 12:10 EXB]; [**ᴸ For] The accuser [ᶜ the name Satan means "**Accuser**" in Hebrew; **Job 1:6–12; 2:1–6; Zech. 3:1–2**] of our **brothers** and **sisters**, who **accused** them day and night **before our God.**

I saw a very similar **dream** in the back year 2015:

"I entered the large church; it seemed to be one of the largest in the world; there wasn't much light, and I walked towards the altar. As I approached the altar, I saw a colossal dragon in front of the altar. The limbs were chained to the walls as if they had been crucified. I felt pretty confident myself, and it seemed that he is so weak. As I stood in front of the dragon, I started to mock him. I was arrogant and the more I mocked, the stronger he got. I got frightened, and I began to rebuke him, and then one of the chains broke, and he grabbed me and lifted me up to his face and started to laugh. I was so frozen.

He began to speak that I considered myself a Christian, but I didn't have power nor authority, etc. He accused and mocked me even worse. I couldn't say anything; I tried to call for Jesus, but I couldn't.

When he continued to speak and said: "... and you're nobody,

> *you are nothing and you are emptiness...” Suddenly I felt a Holy Fire inside of me; something gave me a profound revelation, and I interrupted him: ”NO! You are wrong! I AM A CHILD OF GOD, IM a son OF GOD, and you are nobody, and you don’t have authority over me! As I said it, a powerful explosion ensured with bright light, and he was gone.”*

We need this revelation to ALL!

SECOND VISION

The Holy Spirit told me that I was *“BURNING”* as Maila saw in her dream (*November 10th*). When He said it, it was without fear and sounded in Peace.

Then I saw a *vision* that *“I will burn tonight in our office”*, where I separated myself from the family. Interestingly, I have been drinking so much water today, but only went to the toilet twice, where all the water disappeared?!

This vision scared me, and I thought that my time is up, and I have to say goodbye to my family, without any suspicions to avoid panic among them.

Then I realized that this is about the portal in my backyard, which Maila dreamed of.

I knew that the portal must be closed or I burn.

THIRD VISION

I went to our bedroom where was Maila playing with the tablet and I said to her:*” Please go and pick up our older son from kindergarten, its time (it was about 17:30 / 5:30 p.m.)”* and she replied:

“I will finish my Solitaire first.”

I waited a little time, and then she asked:*” How much fever do you have?”* I replied:*” 39,5 °C (102,2°F)”*, she shook her head and I waited a little bit more, and then I said:" *Please, go right now!"* and then she *"growled"* at me and left.

So I got on my knee in front of my bed, facing towards our backyard and I started to pray, I proclaimed the authority of Jesus Christ, and I took authority over the backyard - I testified that it is Holy ground and bonded the portal!

And then I saw a **vision**: *Heaven opened, and Mighty and Powerful Angel came down with great momentum and landed at His feet so that the earth shook by the blast. Then He took His* **Burning Sword** *from His back and struck it through the portal and destroyed it! And then He flew away.*

I saw Him behind back and distance between us was about 20 meters, after that He didn't say a word, didn't even look at me. The Angel was about 5-7 meters high, and the portal was about three meters: the sword was as the same size as the portal, He struck his sword from above to the ground through the portal and then there was a flash, a blast, an explosion.

Then I received a **Revelation** and the **Word**:

Our fight and the struggle is in prayer so that Heavenly Forces can come and **fight for us; we must take control by declaring** *that the land or ground is under the* **Jurisdiction and Authority of Jesus Christ** *so that it* **allows** *Angels of War to act.*

That's confirmed and illuminated Daniel's fasting in "Daniels 10". The time is right now 18:40 (6:40 p.m.)

"Allegory" – *when I hear that word, it makes me furious in the Holy Spirit! Don't tell me that it all is an "allegory." All things can be "explained through allegory" mindset is wrong, twisted. We use it as an excuse because we don't understand the Spiritual world and what we don't and can't explain, then we just say: "it's a fantasy" to them who believe. Same applies to "Armor of God"* **[Ephesians 6:11-20].** *The Bible consists of many such things, but we have to tell the differences between a song (David's songs) where it is just illustrative, or it's a vision and description of the Spiritual World (like* **the Book of Revelation**). *Our mind*

> *can't handle it: we make our own conclusions based upon our experiences or the pictures that the world has painted for us, a world view that feels secure because we are used to it. Yes –*
> ***secure*** *- all unknown and unreasonable scares us.*
> *Before that, I had the same thinking!*
> *Free your mind!*

21 DECEMBER

I've survived the night, and somehow, I knew that it's not finished yet.
I still feel exhausted and have a strong pain in my chest.

22 DECEMBER   The FINAL BATTLE

FINALE BATTLE

When Maila's sister came to visit, she told me that she saw a bright white flash moving on the second floor, she hinted as it was like an Angel or *"the Good Guys."*

I have felt that it is not a disease or flu, but a pure **ATTACK**, against my heart and my soul; the fever pressurized my heart so heavily, which is full of pain and stabs.
I could feel something in my chest, something moving around. It attacked my heart; I already felt it for two days now.
Suddenly, around 18:00 (6 p.m.), I felt heartsick that I wanted to throw up, and my heart was beating heavily, and I thought that now I am going to die. I went up to my room to lie down to my bed.
I started to cry and shout internally to ABBA, and I thought that I'm insane because I had seen spiritual things and revelation and visions, but did I really?
Then I decided:
I saw it with my eyes **in the spirit** and physical; suddenly I caught

and grabbed it by the head, it was a like 1-meter long snake with a dragon's head, and I started to pull it out from my chest.

When I pulled it out, then I wrapped it between my hands and said: *"I will destroy you and make you void!"* And I throw it in the air, and it was gone – IT WAS SO REAL! And it was real!

> *All these gestures with my hand were real; I had like an x-ray vision. And it all was real!* **I was completely awake and in common sense!** *I saw it as real as I see my two hands, even more realistically, because I also saw the spiritual world in parallel. I can't explain it better.*

And then the **Holy Spirit said:**

> *"It is finished, and now you will* **burn with the Fire of Holy Spirit!"**

This chapter of my life has ended!

… And all the **pain** and **stabs** were gone, and the **freedom** came in **Peace!** My **heart was healed**, and fever dropped.

*And then, the Holy Spirit gave me a **vision** that made me fervent.*

I'll finish **that part of my journey** with my first dream that I had in 2015 when I began to search for a Lord God:

"I saw that **my heart was very sick** and the doctors wanted to give me the heart of a 50 years-old man so that I could live a few years longer. After convincing me, I agreed with heart surgery. I was already on the surgery table, and then they put an anesthesia mask on: **Suddenly**, I shouted that I didn't want surgery anymore. I said that **it's my heart, and God gave me that heart, and I will die with that heart**! But it turned out that my heart was already replaced and I woke up from anesthesia. Everything has already happened, and I didn't realize how fast it happened; I was in shock and didn't satisfy with the situation. But I was already with "**a new heart**", the doctor showed me the old heart and how it looked like. It was so **sick** and **dried up**, etc.

I wanted to keep it as a memory, but I knew I had to let it go!"

When I saw the dream, I was seriously scared that my heart could be sick because my grandfather and his brother had problems with their hearts. My father also admitted that we have to be careful because it could be inheritable heart disease. The fear blinded me years.

But at the beginning of this year, 2020, the Holy Spirit reminded me about that dream and said: "That wasn't about your _physical heart_ that was sick, it was your "_spiritual heart_"!

Because our **Soul** is our **Heart**!

"Above all else, guard your **heart** carefully, because **your life flows** from it." **[Proverbs 4:23 EHV]**

> *"Brothers and sisters, I know that I have **not ·yet reached that goal** [taken hold of it], but there is one thing I always do. **Forgetting the ·past** [ᴸ things that are behind] and **·straining toward** [stretching/reaching forward to] what is ahead, ¹⁴ I keep ·trying to reach **[pursuing; chasing] the goal** and get the **prize** for which God called me ·to the life above [heavenward; ᴸ upward] ·through [or in] Christ Jesus."*
> **[Philippians 3:13-14]**

END OF CHAPTER 1

Perhaps you're wondering what happened to "my warfare with my father," and what happened to the " lottery jackpot?"

First: *About my "warfare" with my father: it was* **April 5, 2020,** *when we had our "ordinary" talk, and we shouted at each other, and suddenly the real reason came out of his heart: He was so disappointed that I lied when I said that* **I will never borrow money from banks or credit companies.** *That was my promise that I broke to pieces. It tore his heart apart, and mine also.*
And I have repented of that and asked forgiveness! And I heard in the spirit, that something broke so loudly, and freedom came back! I got my father back!
Yes, I've lost his trust, but I hope that Lord God can help to heal that wound! But most important that the Peace came!
Father's and son's relationships *are the most complicated and difficult; because there are so many* **expectations** *and* **disappointments.**
Being a father to my own children, I learn every day about the relationship with the heavenly **Father.** *And I thank You, dear ABBA, that you've given me earthly father, who has also been as a guide to Lord Jesus. His blessings and prayers, and also a "warfare" has made me search God more and more.*

Secondly: *About my "affection" for winning the jackpot with the lottery?*
I don't really say that was affection because I know the meaning of the lottery and what comes with that. God knew my heart, that I'm giver, and I believe that not the stupidest giver.
But God asked me:" How can I be **honored** *for this? Who receives* **the glory***? What's the* **benefit** *for me?" Yes – He is like a businessman. He doesn't do things simply; there's always a point, seed to sow. He said that:" Yes, your faith is strong and*

you can win it, but that's not **My Will**; not like this. I will lead and show you the way that is **perfect for you**".

Also, what will happen if I win and people will know that was from the lottery? What **example** I would be? It would be a **disaster, among Christians**. It will grow the "**obsession** (it's not faith) of **free money** from God," the "**health and wealth**" **mindset**. It is already a disaster!

"Not given to everyone- to whom much is given; also much is required of him."

Then I know that I have to stop and give it away to the Lord; I've done it several times, but I have **never repented**. But now I have done it on **April 7, 2020.**

> You ask and do not receive, because you **ask wrongly**, to **spend it on your passions. [James 4:3 ESV]**

We have to remind ourselves that **God is jealous**! And He doesn't **share Glory** with **anybody**! [Exodus 20:5; 34:14]

> [5] Or do you suppose it is to no purpose that the Scripture says, "**He yearns jealously over the spirit that he has made to dwell in us**"? [James 4:5 ESV]

> "I am the LORD. That is my name.
>   **I will not give [share; yield] my glory to another;**
>   I will not let idols take the **praise that should be**
> **mine** [ᴸ my praise]. [Isaiah 42:8]

There is saying that the "***best part must be left to the last***".
So I did, at the end of **that** chapter, I'm sharing <u>my father's
experience</u> that happened about 15 years ago and changed
his life entirely:

MEETING GOD IN COURT

One day I was browsing my medical record, which contains my
history of diseases. I noticed one entry – April 25, 2005. I call that
day as "Great Grace of Lord God"; which fundamentally changed
my attitude to life. I like to share my testimony with you.

It was an ordinary morning. The working day was also quite
typical. I had received from my acquaintance cheek tobacco called
"snus", and I had used it a few times that day. Meanwhile, I also
smoked.
I finished work at about five in the evening. I put tobacco in my
cheek and walked across the road to the bus stop. I saw the bus
coming. Suddenly I felt a cramp under my throat, and my hands
went cold on top, and from the fright, I spat tobacco out of my
mouth before getting on the bus. But it was too late.
Next started "ants" running at my feet. I ran to the front of the bus
because there were few people.
There was no empty seat. The front of my eyes began to blur. I
was standing with my back to the bus front window, and I put both
hands through the armrest on the bus window, facing towards
people.

The fog and the grayness around me deepened.

Suddenly I was in the *Light*. I have never seen such pure and deep Light before. This *Light* was a hundred times whiter than bleached laundry or snow. The mind was still bright; however, all emotions were gone. I didn't feel hot or cold, neither smell. **All the general cognition seems to have disappeared.**

I realized that something severe was happening. It felt like I was facing a **Spirituality** or a creature, but at the same time, *it* was all around me, and *it* didn't have a specific shape. I had no fear.

I remember that standing there in front of that **Spirituality**: I wondered if it's really that simple to go to another world, and it is a matter of seconds? No warnings, no trumpets, no ceremonies. I didn't have any human emotions or feelings, but at the same time, I had the *knowledge* that I have to do something or say something fast. It seemed that a **decision** had to be made immediately.

As being a Christian for 25 years, I thought I would say one prayer right away, and it's all fine. But my head was completely empty. I didn't even remember what prayer meant or how to pray. Then I remembered that during my 25 years as a Christian, being in church and meetings in fellowships, I have prayed "*Our Heavenly Father*" so many times, and I thought I would at least start with that prayer.

But I didn't even remember the first word about that prayer. It seemed that everything human, even memory, didn't work anymore. All weapons *(prayer weapons, knowing good and evil, emotions, etc.)* were taken away from me. But the thinking was perfectly clear, and all the time, when I was standing there, I interacted with that creature in some way.

I still felt that I had to do something. I tried to remember what people have said about their similar experiences. Suddenly I felt that I did not want to move on, but wanted to return to earth.

At that moment, I didn't even think about how good and calm it was there. The first thought was that I had to take care of my son. As the son was an adult and had a covenant with God, I got the answer; that is settled. And then I thought I had to take care of my parents - I was told that everything would be fine with them as well. Then I wanted to know with whom my Son is going to marry-

I got an answer that it will be ok also.

I wanted to see my grandchildren, but I felt that I shouldn't worry about them either.

Then I wondered to myself how much *good* I had accomplished while I had been a believer.

At that thought, I was asked how much I had done bad things during my living years.

Obviously, I didn't discuss that topic further in my thought. I was cornered.

I thought it couldn't be that there's no way to go back. Getting here was so easy and fast.

Is there really nothing that can be fixed? After all, the car can be repaired if it breaks.

Even if you've told someone something bad, insulting, it can be fixed – ask for forgiveness.

Every situation in life can be changed or fixed. It just can't be *"the end"* of it all at once.

The answer to my thoughts was very clear and straightforward: **yes, it is that simple.**

There's nothing that you can do anymore.

That answer shocked me. But I didn't give up. All I could do was that I went to the elderly in my mind, whose sincere **faith** I have seen in their **actions**. I wondered what they would do if they wanted something to change. But they're calling the name of Jesus! I was a Christian for 25 years, but I had forgotten that **Jesus** is the way to God. I considered that prayer ends with the name of Jesus, somehow too obvious and ordinary. I had never gone deeper into that true meaning. I had God but didn't have Christ.

As soon as I spoke the name of Jesus, there was a rumble. That surprised me, but my mouth continued to pronounce the name of Jesus. I repeated this continuously until I finally shouted the name of Jesus. The rumble intensified, it felt like a strong wind, but there wasn't any movement around me.

Suddenly a very large and thick book appeared in front of me to the right corner.

The book was open. Without realizing anything, I saw the pages of the book moved as if someone was browsing. Suddenly the browsing ended, and the book remained open in one place.

I felt that someone was reading this book loudly. I don't remember if I read it along with a loud voice, or I did so in spirit. But I agreed in my mind with the reader. One moment I saw that the book was closed, but the *Light* was still around me. Somehow I realized that everything was over, and I could go back to the world. But now I was as offended by it. I thought **could it be so easy** - before I was told that I couldn't go back. So, after calling Jesus' name and reading the Book of Life, suddenly going back was possible? If before communication with the creature had taken place without talking, now I suddenly heard a clear and loud voice that said: **"yes, it's that simple."** The voice that came from near me sounded rough and a little bit grumpy.

The understanding from where the voice came, I leave it to myself. In the future, that will give me the opportunity to check if people are telling the truth when they claim that God has spoken to them personally or not.

The next moment I felt myself hanging on the same armrest in the front of the bus and saw how the bright *Light* became more and more hazy and gray. Finally, people's shapes reappeared, and I realized that I'm still on the bus. I rather not describe the expressions on the faces of the passengers. Perhaps they were frightened that I screamed the name of Jesus. I don't know what the person next to me experienced or saw at the same time. Maybe they thought that I was a drunk or a drug addict. I don't know what they were really thinking and what they had seen and heard.

I immediately got off the bus. I noticed that I had passed two bus stops. I called my family doctor, who asked me to come and to take a cardiogram the next day. I can tell you, for now, that cardiogram showed that I had a risk of a heart attack. Further examination revealed that I had a thrombus. After I got off from the bus, I realized what really happened to me. I was shocked. I had a panic fear. And I still couldn't believe that I'm back in the world. It all was real.

A note confirms this on the printout of my cardiogram. When

someone asks me today if you believe that God exists, I look at him incomprehensibly, because I know, and I am convinced that He exists. How can you doubt the existence of fire if you have put your hand in the fire and got burned? Do not doubt that God exists. I must disappoint the Christians, who think that maybe He still does not exist and live in self-deception. **GOD IS REAL.**
I learned from this experience that no one could ask me anymore what the meaning of life is.
Whenever a believer is asked what the meaning of his life is, then the answer is quite uncertain.
I remember how pastor Rein Uuemõis has advised his congregation to become full of faith and the Holy Spirit. That experience on the bus showed me that if we stand in the *Light*, all the weapons that we are used in this world will be taken: cognition (senses), the power of prayer, the word of God, our experiences. There's not possible to justify yourself when you stand before God - explain why I acted like did in different situations. For example, look, what that person did to me, so that's why I did it to him. These all are facts only.
What motivated you (anger, jealousy, etc.) doesn't really matter.
I believe that one of the reasons why they send me back is to tell others about this experience.
The second reason was that; God showed that without the blood of the Son's sacrifice, no contract will be made that leads to the Salvation. It was a direct warning that people would not forget the role of the Son: He is the gateway to God. Unfortunately, I forgot that truth, during my 25 -year walk of faith. There were also other things that I learned, but they were meant just for me. Remember that, when you stand in the court, you are completely helpless, and you don't have the power to change something. It doesn't matter if you've been a believer for 50 years or done something *good*. It counts only what is inside of you and what flows out of you while you stand before the court.

> "If anyone believes in me, **rivers of living water** will flow out from that person's **heart** [*L* belly; gut], as the Scripture says [*Is. 55:1; 58:11; Ezek. 47:1–12; Zech. 14:8*, compare *John 4:10–11; Rev. 7:17; 22:1*]." **[John 7:38]**

One consolation is that when you are in court, you have a lawyer who will answer for you, speak for you, and apologize for you. I would like to give a life-based example: One day I saw a movie about Mother Teresa: The documentary called "*Mother Teresa – Saint of darkness.*" There was also an interview with her confessor, as we know, Teresa was a Catholic. The confessor read aloud a passage from her mother Teresa's correspondence. In one letter, Mother Teresa had confessed that she had served God for 40 years, but God had forsaken her. What a shock it can be for people who die, but have never done God's will and walked in His ways.

> "Not all those who say [*L* to me] 'You are our Lord' [*L* 'Lord! Lord!'] will enter the kingdom of heaven, **but only those who do what my Father in heaven wants** [the **will of my Father** in heaven]. **22** On the last day [judgment day; *L* that day] many people will say to me, 'Lord, Lord, we spoke for you [*L* Did we not prophesy in your name…?], and through you we forced out demons [*L* cast out demons in your name…?] and did many miracles [*L* mighty works in your name…?].' **23** Then I will tell them clearly [declare to them; publicly announce to them], 'I never knew you. Get away [Depart] from me, you who do evil [break God's law; practice lawlessness; *Ps. 6:8*].'" **[Matthew 7:21-23]**

> *The world and everything that people want in it [^{L} its
> desire/lust] are passing away [1 Cor. 7:31], but the **person who
> does what God wants** [the **will of God**] **lives** [abides;
> remains] **forever. [1 John 2:17]**

The Word of God also says that God's grace is justified through faith. Also, the Word of God says that the **secret of the faith is in clear conscience [1 Timothy 3:9].**

Thinking of that experience, I'm glad that it happened to me. I later spoke to an acquaintance that had been in clinical condition as a result of a heart attack. Doctors brought him back.

I asked him to describe his experience. He said he had been in a tunnel, gray all around.

Gray hairballs moved along with him in the tunnel. Meanwhile, large black paws appeared that took away those hairballs. I asked if he could see the end of the tunnel. He said that all he could see was that the tunnel that split into two at one point but was brought back here before he had reached that point. I told him never to choose gray, just choose the *Light*. But at the same time, I realized that decision wasn't him to make at that point. I'm glad my experience was different - I was immediately brought to the *Light*.

So I still have hope!

CHAPTER 2

The **beginning** of **Your new** chapter starts now!

---

*"In the **midst of the trial**, you can write the **triumphant**, that you can be a more than a **conqueror** because you have **victory** in the **midst of the strife**."*

THANK YOU

Thank you for your time!
I especially thank my wife, parents, Anre Matetski, and Meelis Etti senior for their support.